$\mathcal{E}$ver since a group of farmers established an electric cooperative in 1937 and brought electricity to outlying farms, Connexus Energy has brightened the lives of Anoka County residents by providing reliable and affordable electricity. Deeply rooted in the community, we are a proud sponsor of *Picturing Anoka County: 150 Years of Anoka County History*.

$\mathcal{M}$ercy and Unity Hospitals are proud to sponsor this history on behalf of the citizens of Anoka County in appreciation for the community's trust and support as patients, family members, employees, physicians, volunteers, and donors. It is our pleasure to serve the people of Anoka County as the county celebrates its 150th anniversary. Congratulations!

MERCY & UNITY
HOSPITALS
Allina Hospitals & Clinics

$\mathcal{V}$illage Bank, born and raised in Anoka County, with five offices and more than $200 million in assets, is a proud sponsor of the Anoka County Historical Society and of this limited edition history. We congratulate the County on 150 years of growth and prosperity, and we thank the members of the Historical Society for their dedication to collecting, preserving, and telling our story.

Picturing Anoka County:

150 Years of Anoka County History

Sharron Stockhausen

Photo editors: Todd Mahon and Vickie Wendel

THE
DONNING COMPANY
PUBLISHERS

Left: *Anoka County Farm Bureau Association officers and directors in 1949. Front row (l-r): Vice President Charles Wickstrom, Director Mrs. Willard Hanks, President L. O. Jacob, Home and Community Chair Mrs. C. C. Perkins, and Secretary J. R. Meister. Back row: Blaine Farm Bureau Unit President Freeman Meister, Director Ralph Westberg, Anoka Unit President Victor Hodson, Minnesota Farm Bureau Federation President Frank White, Director George Giddings, Burns unit President Lloyd Wirz, Anoka County Youth Group President and Director R. J. Beckenbach. The Farm Bureau began in Minnesota in 1913 when farmers, realizing the need for an effective voice in agricultural policy, began to organize. Their mission was to advocate for agriculture based on the beliefs of its members.* **Right:** *Troop 2 of the Girl Scouts attended Cutters Camp on Round Lake in 1929. Pictured are Evadena Ricketts, Hannah Sell, unknown, Miss Sylvester, and Betty Weaver.*

The Donning Company Publishers
184 Business Park Drive, Suite 206
Virginia Beach, VA 23462-6533

Steve Mull, General Manager
Barbara Buchanan, Office Manager
Kathleen Sheridan, Senior Editor
Stephanie Danko, Graphic Designer
Mellanie Denny, Imaging Artist
Scott Rule, Director of Marketing
Stephanie Linneman, Marketing Coordinator
Lori Kennedy, Project Research Coordinator

Steve Mull, Project Director

Library of Congress Cataloging-in-Publication Data
Stockhausen, Sharron.
  Picturing Anoka County : 150 years of Anoka county history / Sharron Stockhausen ; Todd Mahon and Vickie Wendel, photo editors.
     p. cm.
  Includes index.
  ISBN–13: 978-1-57864-377-6
  ISBN–10: 1-57864-377-5
  1. Anoka County (Minn.)—History. 2. Anoka County (Minn.)—History—Pictorial works. 3. Anoka County (Minn.)—Social conditions.
4. Anoka County (Minn.)—Economic conditions. I. Mahon, Todd. II. Wendel, Vickie. III. Title.
  F612.A6S76 2006
  977.6'65—dc22

                                        2006028673

Published in the United States of America by Walsworth Publishing Company

Table of Contents

Foreword

*A*noka County has a rich and diverse history–a history that is still in the making. We are living history and making history here. The photos and descriptions in this book remind us how important it is that we record and document the progress, change, and decisions being made now that will one day be part of our history.

Over the past 150 years, our communities have been able to change and adapt to different ways of life and commercial activities–from ox carts and the trade of pelts; to the timber industry and use of the Mississippi and Rum Rivers to float the logs down river for milling; to agriculture and the use of wagons, and later trucks, for hauling produce to the cities; to our current mix of housing, commercial districts, and small and large businesses with commuters driving their own vehicles, and soon riding Northstar Commuter Rail, to and from their places of work.

Ingenuity, adaptability, innovation, hard work, and coming together as a community to accomplish goals have run deep throughout our Anoka County tradition.

As you look through these pages, reflect on the fact that you, too, are part of Anoka County's rich heritage. What photos and descriptions will the residents of the next 150 years recall of our own impact on the growth and development of this proud community?

Margaret Langfeld
Chair of the Anoka County Board of Commissioners

Acknowledgments

The Anoka County Historical Society wishes to express its sincerest gratitude to everyone who has been instrumental in the publication of this book.

First and foremost, we thank the sponsors:
- Village Bank—with special thanks to Don and Jamie Kveton, the staff, and the Board of Directors
- Connexus Energy
- Mercy and Unity Hospitals (part of Allina Hospitals and Clinics).

We also thank those who donated their photographs to the ACHS collections over the years out of a generosity of spirit and love for history. Putting this project together has allowed us to increase the volume and variety of images in the collection, and many of these photos are found within the pages of this book. Thank you to Steven and Carol Hunstperger; Julie Shortridge and Marty Doll of Anoka County; John VonDeLinde and Jennifer Fink from Anoka County Parks and Recreation; Lou Paulson; Ruth Nelson and Linda Johnson from the City of Hilltop; Julie Jones from the City of Fridley; Lynn Wendel; Ron Wendel; Becky Loader and the Columbia Heights Library Collection; Carol Larson and the Anoka Technical College; Mary Alice Divine and the City of Lino Lakes; the staff of the City of Spring Lake Park; and the staff of the City of Circle Pines.

From my side of the desk, Sharron Stockhausen seemed effortless in her work. It was a great pleasure to get to know her better during this process. Her sense of professionalism, expertise in publishing, and knowledge of the subject matter made her more than an author—and also a needed advisor and confidant.

Kathie Bomista was kind enough to proofread both the manuscript for the text and the initial draft for the photo captions.

Ellen Green gave helpful advice early in the process and provided a map for starting the project.

The Anoka County Board of Commissioners has been unbelievably supportive of both the Historical Society and the Anoka County sesquicentennial celebration. Without their financial support, none of this would be possible.

The Anoka County Historical Society Board of Directors deserves untold amounts of credit for guiding the organization to ever-increasing levels of visibility and credibility. Members of the current board are responsible for a successful capital campaign and continue to establish policies and represent the organization throughout the county. They share a debt of gratitude to those in the past who gave their time and expertise by serving as board members.

Vickie Wendel, ACHS Program Manager, was the gentle but firm hand over the selection of the photographs. Vickie's commitment to representing the entire county made this a much better book. Her work to preserve and share Anoka County's history is a benefit to all who have lived and worked in the county. Her extensive knowledge of Anoka County's history is certainly unmatched.

Bonnie McDonald served as the Executive Director for ACHS during the earliest days of planning for the sesquicentennial. Her vision helped guide the process, and we are still benefiting from her contributions.

The Sesquicentennial Executive Board is responsible for the planning of the 150th anniversary celebration. It was with their approval that this project moved forward. We thank them for their commitment to celebrating Anoka County's wonderful past and exciting future.

Thank you to everyone we could not name. Trust that we thought of you all but may have missed some of you, and for that we apologize.

Finally, a special thank you goes to everyone who has contributed to Anoka County's history in his or her own way. Some of their names are recorded in this book and other publications, but most of them are not. While their names may not be recorded in history, their efforts and impact on the county are seen in the wonderful communities we call home. Thank you to all of Anoka County's residents.

Inevitably, there will be some omissions, misinterpretations, and outright errors in a volume like this. We take full responsibility for those and take seriously correcting them for the public record.

Todd Mahon
Anoka County Historical Society, Executive Director

Picturing Anoka County:
150 Years of Anoka County History

by Sharron Stockhausen, MMA

Anoka, although an unusual moniker, serves as an appropriate descriptor of the area that bears its name. In the Dakota Indian language, Anoka means "on both sides." Anoka, the county seat, spans both sides of the Rum River and lies at the confluence of the Mississippi and Rum Rivers. In the Ojibwa language, Anoka belongs to a phrase that means "work on the water."

The water proved to be important to Anoka County history as European-descended settlers bought water rights to use in their saw mills, flour mills, and everything else that could use water to generate power.

Early on, the area served as neutral ground between the Dakota and Chippewa. French traders saw the value in using the locale to trade with both nations since neither was expected to occupy the area for a lengthy time. Neutral territory was typically more secure than claimed territory, so the traders settled in, believing their goods were safe from robbery or pillaging.

The book, *History of Anoka County and the Towns of Champlin and Dayton in Hennepin County Minnesota*, authored by Albert M. Goodrich and published by the Hennepin Publishing Company in 1905, then republished by the Anoka Bicentennial Commission in 1976, offers an account of the Battle of Rum River. The book says in spring 1839 eight hundred Chippewa, including men, women, and children, assembled at Fort Snelling to receive payment they believed they had coming.

They were not paid, however, so decided to return home—some headed toward the Mississippi River and others toward the St. Croix. There were Sioux (Dakota) living in the Fort Snelling area who visited the Chippewa and were invited to stay and enjoy feasting and dancing.

On July 1, the Chippewa began their journey home. Unfortunately, two of the young men, whose father had been slain by a Sioux during the previous year's visit, were overcome with grief after visiting their father's grave and took revenge on a Sioux known as Badger by scalping him. Badger's body was found, wrapped in a blanket, and brought home to the Sioux.

Yeetkadootah, one of Badger's relatives, swore revenge and headed up a party to follow the Chippewa and avenge Badger's death.

The Chippewa weren't expecting any trouble as they headed up the Mississippi River toward home. Most likely, they were unaware of what the two young Chippewa did to Badger. They made camp on the northwest side of Round Lake in Anoka County.

The morning of July 4, the Sioux attacked the sleeping Chippewa and killed them where they lay. Goodrich's book reports approximately ninety Chippewa died that day in 1839.

In the 1840s, the French set up a trading post in the modern-day community of Ramsey. Then in 1849, the Minnesota territorial legislature organized three counties—Washington, Ramsey, and Benton—in the Anoka County area. The Rum River served as the boundary between Ramsey and Benton Counties.

As more settlers began arriving, the Indian word Anoka came into common use. In 1856, Sherburne County broke away from Benton County. The land east of Sherburne and west of the Rum River then became part of Ramsey County. Per legislative action, Anoka County was officially formed on May 23, 1857, a year before Minnesota statehood.

Anoka County's original eight townships were Anoka, Watertown (known today as Ramsey), Round Lake Township (known today as Andover), Bethel, Columbus, St. Francis, Oak Grove, and Centerville.

The county took up the same territory then as it does now, with one exception. The same day Anoka County was created, a small portion of land bordering the Mississippi River along the southeastern tip of the current county boundary was also created into a county named Manomin. The tiny space contained what we know today as Columbia Heights, Fridley, Hilltop, and Spring Lake Park. It occupied one-third of a congressional township and functioned as an organized township for more than twelve years. It was then attached to Anoka County by constitutional amendment on November 2, 1869. But it kept the name Manomin another ten years. In 1879, Manomin changed its name to Fridley.

In 2007, Anoka County boasts eighteen incorporated cities and two townships. Note that eleven of the county's cities were formed in 1974. That's because a state legislative act changed the status of Anoka County villages to cities.

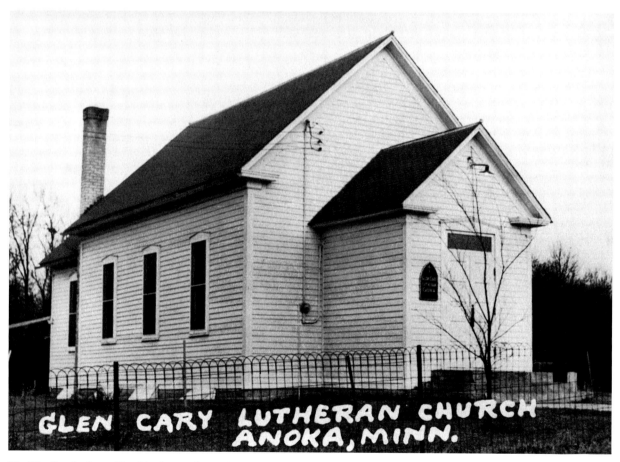

The Glen Cary Lutheran Church in the area that would eventually be known as Ham Lake, undated.

Community	Formation History
Andover	First called Round Lake, then Grow, then Andover. Township formed in 1857. City formed in 1974.
Anoka	City formed in 1878 after several early attempts to make it a city were voted down by voters.
Bethel	Began as a township. Village formed in 1899. City formed in 1974.
Blaine	Township formed in 1877. City formed in 1964.
Burns Township	Township separated from St. Francis Township in 1869.
Centerville	Platted in 1854. Village formed in 1910, city in 1974.
Circle Pines	Village formed in 1950. City formed in 1974.
Columbia Heights	Part of Manomin originally, then township. Village formed in 1898. City formed in 1921.
Columbus	Township formed in 1857. Incorporated as a city in 2006.
Coon Rapids	Part of Anoka Township originally. Coon Creek dam construction 1898–1914 created small community. Village formed in 1952. City formed in 1959.
East Bethel	Known as township of Bethel when village of Bethel formed in 1899. Village formed in 1957. City formed in 1974.
Fridley	Part of Manomin originally. Annexed to Anoka County in 1870 and known as Manomin Township. Named Fridley Township in 1879. Village formed in 1949. City formed in 1957.
Ham Lake	Village formed in 1973. City formed in 1974.
Hilltop	Village formed in 1956. City formed in 1974.
Lexington	Village formed in 1950. City formed in 1974.
Lino Lakes	Part of Centerville Township originally. Village formed in 1955. City formed in 1974.
Linwood Township	Part of Bethel and Columbus originally. Township formed in 1871.
Oak Grove	Township formed in 1857. City formed in 1993.
Ramsey	First called Watertown, then Dover, then Ramsey. City formed in 1974.
St. Francis	Township formed in 1857. Village formed in 1962. City formed in 1974.
Spring Lake Park	Village formed in 1953. City formed in 1973. Part of city resides in Ramsey County.

As the immigrants came from Germany, Sweden, Norway, Poland, and Ireland, they tended to settle in communities with other homeland immigrants. Burns Township boasted a Swedish population. Centerville was home to the French Canadians. The Columbia Heights population came from Poland. The Irish made their homes in Oak Grove (Cedar). Ham Lake became home to those who came from Norway and Sweden, while those from Germany tended to settle in Lino Lakes. The county seat, Anoka, held several ethnic neighborhoods—one was even called "Swede Town."

During the past 150 years, Anoka County's population has continually grown. From 1990 to 2000, the population increased 22.3 percent. Four years later, in 2004, it increased another 7.3 percent, according to the U.S. Census Bureau. While the breakout for each nationality, such as German, is not available, the Census Bureau reports that in 2000, 92.8 percent of the Anoka County population is White (not Latino), 1.6 percent is Black, 0.7 percent is Native American, and 1.7 percent is Asian, and 1.7 percent is Latino. The remaining 1.5 percent reported they are of mixed race. Foreign-born residents made up a mere 3.6 percent of Anoka County's residents in the year 2000.

One of Anoka County's communities doesn't carry a formal designation, but it's a community all the same. Two years before Minnesota became a state, settlers platted a piece of land they called Glencarie, or as we know it today, Glen Cary. There's a discrepancy in the number of shanties that were built as the foundation for the settlement, but either seven or eight of the makeshift structures framed the section that was advertised as a future city. Within a year of the settlement's start, a prairie fire raced through the area, leveling the shanties and destroying the dream of having a city on the prairie. After the fire, several settlers came forward and made claims on the land. On February 21, 1871, the Anoka County commissioners separated the homesteads from Grow Township and formed the community of Ham Lake.

Another unofficial Anoka County community is the area currently known as Johnsville. It began as a remote school for grades one through five in 1893 and almost blew away forty years later. By the 1920s, some entrepreneurs began building their homes and businesses in the Johnsville area, a part of Blaine Township. They had hardly gotten their roots down when a huge storm almost flattened the area in 1925. When that horror passed, nothing resembled the buildings and homes that once stood. Henry Trost and John Augustson owned a garage and a grocery store in the little community, but the storm shredded their business and almost sent Johnsville into oblivion. As has happened so often in Anoka County, the determined spirit of the people prevailed, and Trost and Augustson rebuilt their businesses.

Inspired by the tenacity of these two men, others came to the area and began building their homes. As the population grew, talk of naming the area started to spread. Since it was in the Blaine Township, there was a discussion to name it Blaine. Instead, to honor the man who remained faithful to rebuilding his business in the area, the name Johnsville, after John Augustson, was adopted. Many people think only of the Johnsville school when they hear the name. That seems fitting since an 1893 school started the little community.

Anoka County residents have always enjoyed the ability to get around both on land and by water navigation. One of the earliest land transportation modes was the Red River Valley oxcarts. The unoiled wooden axles turned wooden wheels, which made a high-pitched screeching sound, alerting everyone around that the oxcarts were on the trail.

The earliest carts used wheels made of solid discs of wood that had no spokes. The discs were five feet in diameter and about three inches thick. Absolutely no metal was used in their construction. Only wooden pegs and rawhide thongs held them together. Later versions of the carts used wheels that had spokes and rims, but still no metal was used. The tires were braided rawhide that was woven about the wheel rims. No oil or grease was allowed on the axles. The dust and noise that the wheels kicked up were almost

Red River Trail oxcart, 1820–60. Trains of up to three hundred of these carts passed through Anoka in its early days.

unbearable. As many as three hundred carts made up one single train. Each cart carried about five hundred pounds of fur hides.

The drivers of these carts, many of whom were half-Canadian, were known as *bois brulés* (which means wood-burned or scorched) because of their browned complexions. They ate pemmican, a rich and highly spiced concoction of shredded buffalo meat laced with tallow in casings made from untanned buffalo hides. Some said the pemmican was rancid, unattractive, and offensive, but the *bois brulés* disagreed.

In the 1880s, people traveled from city to city in stagecoaches. One primary route took travelers from St. Paul to Duluth and points north of there. A main stop on the route was Kettle River Junction, a crossroads community known today as Lino Lakes. Today the stagecoach route is known as Highway 8 (it was added to maps in 1928, the year the road was paved), but even before it had a name, the road was of supreme importance as a main artery used by stagecoaches. As they carried passengers and cargo, stagecoaches and wagons fought their way through deep ruts in the hard soil. The ruts were left by those coaches whose wheels passed through muddy surfaces, and the tracks they left later dried in the hot sun.

Kettle River Junction may have been only a trail, but the soft sand of the area blew into the deep ruts and allowed stagecoaches to get back on track as they pulled through the sand-filled ruts. The original post office in the Lino Lakes area was established in 1894 and had only one postmaster, Mr. Parks, before it closed. The post office enjoyed a very short life.

When Anoka County residents clustered into small communities, one of the things they hoped for was a railroad connection to St. Paul and St. Anthony. Their dream came closer when the St. Paul and Pacific Railroad completed the connection between St. Paul and St. Anthony in 1862. Once those two locations were joined, the railroad began to look west toward St. Cloud. In spring 1863, grading began on the railroad bed through what is now known as Fridley (but was known as Manomin

County in those days). By December 6, 1863, trains carried passengers from St. Paul to Manomin, and by December 9, the trains could go on to Coon Creek (currently known as Coon Rapids). Since the train could not turn around at Coon Creek, any trains venturing that far had to run backwards to Manomin to use the turntable.

The railroad ordered more than one hundred thousand railroad ties for the new line between St. Paul and St. Cloud, and the men worked hard to make the new line happen. By December 10, the track was just two miles east of Anoka. Four days later, passenger trains traveled the new line. Watching the railroad's progress, the *Anoka Star* reported, "Railroad pushing along. There is, no doubt, iron enough to finish the railroad into Anoka." On December 12, the *Star* reported the good news: "The whistle of the engine is now heard in Anoka. An event long waited and wished for. We should prepare for a grand jubilee when the cars arrive in town." On Saturday, January 9, 1864, the newspaper reported, "First through train—We had the gratification Monday of being the first to enter the car, which arrived and was the first to depart from Anoka. It was a moment of proud satisfaction. An event long waited for, but no less gratifying since the thing is accomplished."

As the Great Northern Railway pushed its way out from the big city, it helped small communities pop up along the way. A little community was forming near Highway 65 on the eastern boundary of the old Grow Township. In 1899, a post office was built to serve the growing population. The original postmaster, O. A. Johnson, was tasked with naming the little community. As a man who liked to have a reason for what he did, Johnson named the settlement after his daughter, Constance. The reason he named his daughter Constance is that he served on the ship *Constantinople*. The little community never grew much beyond the confines of its original settlement, however, so on March 1, 1955, the post office closed for the last time. In its day, Constance boasted a community church, a schoolhouse, and the Constance Grange. First organized in 1935 with twenty-five members, the new Grange Hall was built in 1940. The Constance Grange worked on community projects, involved itself in educational endeavors, and acted as a social gathering place.

One small Anoka County community that began as a railroad section house is Cedar. Most of its residents were connected with the railroad in some way. The Cedar post office was established for those wanting to communicate with loved ones. Eventually, the area grew, and more people claimed Cedar as home. The community needed a name, so it took the name of Cedar, after a nearby stream, Cedar Creek. Quickly becoming known for its cooperative inhabitants, Cedar became a desirable place to live. Area farmers brought their teams together to build good roads. Locals teamed up to drain the wet, boggy lands and reclaim them for use. The farmers worked with the townsfolk to build the first store, named the Farmers' General Store. In 1908, the Cedar Commercial Club was built as a place people could meet, socialize, and enjoy themselves. In 1917, townspeople joined with farmers and bought stock to form the Farmers' State Bank of Cedar. Clearly, the community worked together to get things done.

Another community that needed to get something done was late-nineteenth-century Coon Creek. One of Anoka County's well-known residents, Irving A. Caswell, was born at Coon Creek on February 25, 1870. Caswell became Anoka's postmaster and an editor of the *Anoka Herald*. On January 1, 1941, at age seventy, Caswell reminisced about his life in the early days of Coon Creek and wrote that transportation in the 1870s wasn't what it was in the 1940s. He described the roads as unpaved "wagon trails through the groves." He also claimed, "All pupils had to walk to school, some of them more than three miles." Caswell also wrote about the steamboat *Monticello.* It was a side-wheeler that traveled the Mississippi River. He recalled the steamboat "was often delayed for hours by the rocks of Coon Rapids." Along with the steamboat, people used the daily stagecoach to travel between Anoka and Minneapolis along the East River Road, formerly known as the U.S. Military Trail and the Red River Trail. Caswell finished his account by telling that "Beginning in April of each year and continuing through most of the summer, there was a continuous procession of emigrants westward bound in canvas covered vehicles."

Caswell didn't say anything about the push to dam up the river in Coon Creek, however. On February 8, 1898, the *Anoka Herald* reported, "The big scheme [to dam the Mississippi River below Coon Creek] is not now only possible, but probable." *The Anoka Union* reported on August 3, 1898, that a "new dam at Coon Creek will be located about a mile and a half below Coon Creek. Surveys are being made in the vicinity and it is thought the work will begin within a year." Things went a little slower than anticipated. First, the location of the dam had to be decided. John Dunn's land was most desirable, but his land was some of the richest in the county, and he didn't want to lose it. Finally, during October 1909, word got out that the Great Northern Development Company of Duluth had been discreetly buying small parcels of land on both sides of the Mississippi River for the dam project. It was one of the best-kept secrets in the county. On October 6, 1909, the newspaper reported, "The proposed dam project at Coon Rapids to harness the Mississippi River and generate some ten thousand horsepower now seems to be an assured fact."

Once the land was purchased, plans for the dam were expedited. The powerhouse belonged at the narrowest portion of the river where the current was most swift. John Dunn finally sold 169 acres of his land for the dam site. Discussions ensued about Anoka County getting the dam and Hennepin County, across the river, getting the energy. In December 1912, fifty men were hired to begin construction. A village sprung up around the dam site. The men and their families lived on-site. Bunkhouses, mess halls, a school, a hospital, a sewer system, and even a thirty-branch telephone exchange took over the village. As with other area communities, the dam village had weddings, births, deaths, parties, and some crime and fire disasters. At the pinnacle of the construction, more than a thousand men worked on the dam. On March 15, 1913, Northern States Power acquired a federal permit, flowage rights, and the land and water powers. Within ten days, it sold its rights to the Northern Mississippi River Power Company so it could finish the hydro development. Community residents expect certain services to be provided, and Anoka County communities did their best to meet those expectations.

Before Bethel became a community, four Quaker families arrived in Anoka County and settled near modern-day Bethel. Originally, the settlement was called the Quaker settlement. About the time the Quakers arrived, James Cooper also came to the settlement and built his home. The area became known as Cooper's Corner, and is called that to this day. Cooper thought of a more original name for the new township that formed in 1858. He chose the name Bethel from the Bible because it means "the House of God." As Bethel grew, Cooper's Corner kept its own identity. The first store and first school opened in 1876. Few other buildings were erected in the little hamlet, but that was just fine with the residents since agriculture was the community's primary industry. The farmers sold their crops of potatoes to the marketplace in Minneapolis. As the soil wore out, the ever-flexible farmers turned their land into dairy farms. When the postal service came through in 1863, Cooper was appointed postmaster. Since there were so few families in the early settlement, he needed only a small flip-top desk to sort out the mail for the residents. Today the Cooper's Corner "post office" resides at the Anoka County History Center. A 1904 map of Anoka County lists landowners plus acreage owned. It also gives the locations of county schools and their district numbers, churches, cemeteries, and even rural post offices.

Anoka not only boasted a busy post office, but in its history it has been known for its excellent library.

At the time the map was created, Blaine had a rural post office located on Blaine Township, Section 6, named "Tuthill Post Office." The map shows that C. D. Tuthill owned a 120-acre parcel with a building on it (perhaps the building was his home) and the post office. He owned an additional 164 acres just north of that location as well. Born in Newberg, New York, in March 1832, Tuthill came to Minnesota and settled in Dodge County. In 1861, he enlisted with Company B, 10th Minnesota Infantry and was shot in the leg before he ever left the northern states. He tried to move on with his company despite his wound, but got only as far as St. Louis, Missouri, when he had to return to Fort Snelling because of his injury. Eventually, he married, became a probate judge, and moved to Fridley in 1882 and to Blaine nine years later. He lived there with his wife, three sons, and a daughter. He went on to serve on the Blaine Town Board, and, in 1897, the Blaine post office was established and he was appointed postmaster. There is speculation he may have had some say in naming the new post office. On January 30, 1904, the Tuthill Post Office was discontinued, and mail was sent to Anoka.

Anoka not only boasted a busy post office, but in its history it has been known for its excellent library. In 1859, some forward-thinking members of Anoka tried to start a library. They gave their money and asked others for money and books. As their collection grew, they rented a small room, set up regular business hours, and the library became a reality. As the community grew, however, so did the need to use the library room for other purposes. A local photographer, J. M. Woods, offered to house the library in his apartments, so the library moved. There wasn't any money to pay a librarian, so it was hard to keep track of where the books were and when they were due back. By 1870, Woods' growing business needed the space that housed the books. With no other options, the library books were donated to the public schools. Ten years later, a group's efforts to reestablish the public library were unsuccessful. Another twelve years passed before anything else was done. In 1892, the *Anoka Union* published an article supporting the idea of a public library. Mrs. J. H. Niles of the Philolectian Society encouraged the group to take on the project. The city council levied a one-mill tax to fund the new endeavor, and the mayor appointed a nine-member library board. The board rented rooms at the corner of Main Street and Second Avenue. Nearly five hundred books were donated, and almost a thousand more were purchased. Another seventeen hundred congressional records and public documents came from Senator C. K. Davis. Mrs. Rose was appointed librarian to oversee the whole thing. The library officially opened in 1894 with more than eight hundred pieces checked out every month. Ten years later, that number doubled to sixteen hundred.

Today the Anoka Public Library is part of the Anoka County Library system. The county library system began with a declaration in 1956 outlining the status and projected need for library services in the county. At the time, only two libraries existed in the county—Anoka and Columbia Heights both maintained city libraries. Over the following decades, the Anoka County Library opened locations throughout the county. The 1990s brought increasing population to Anoka County, and the greater demand for library services fostered discussions of merging the Anoka City Library with the Anoka County libraries. On January 1, 1995, the merger took place. On the other hand, the Columbia Heights Public Library opened its doors in the theater building in 1928 and remains Anoka County's only city library.

Fire was a constant concern in communities. J. P. Woodbury built his mill on the west back of the Rum River in St. Francis in 1891. Located about one hundred feet below the bridge that crossed the river, the mill did a booming business until the early 1920s. After it ceased operation, the mill stood as a proud landmark and reminder of former times. The four-story frame building served as a warehouse for the mill machinery after its productive days were over. On July 18, 1933, Mrs. R. G. Streetly glanced toward the Woodbury mill and thought something was wrong. She looked closer and saw the mill was on fire. She yelled, "Fire! Fire! The mill's on fire!" The men visiting C. H. Shaw's store rushed to the fire scene. They were shocked at how quickly the fire burned through the wooden structure. Dense clouds of smoke reached into the sky. Many of the embers landed more than four hundred feet from the scene. Because of the flying embers and the intense heat, firefighters couldn't get any closer than the four-hundred-foot perimeter. By 8:30 p.m., the fire had burned through the main building supports, and the mill crumbled to the ground. Sparks from the falling building flew onto the bridge that crossed the Rum River and began to set it on fire. Although the fire lasted more than six hours and was reported as "the hottest [fire] that St. Francis had ever had," the town was spared.

Law enforcement officers served as an integral part of each community. The book *Columbia Heights: Bootstrap Town (A Social History)* by Irene Parsons chronicled the Columbia Heights Police Department. Columbia Heights had no formal law enforcement for its first seven years of existence. In 1905, August Beurger was paid one dollar for one day of constable service. In 1919, Gust Holms was special constable, and his biggest job was keeping people from cutting ice from the village skating ponds. The next year, the constable received payment for using his personal car for police work. Then, in 1921, things got really busy. The Parent Teacher Association (PTA) and the Commercial Club lobbied to have a curfew law enforced. Police officers began street patrol from 8:00 p.m. to midnight. For this extra work, they received fifty cents per hour. In July of that same year, Fred West landed the job of special officer for regulating automobile speeders. The next year, 1922, the council earmarked four hundred dollars to purchase a motorcycle for officer Jake Heller. Heller, however, could have the motorcycle only if he kept it in gas and in good repair.

One of the things that was not in good repair in Anoka County the year Minnesota attained statehood was the liquor industry. The year Minnesota won its statehood is the year the temperance movement cleaned up Anoka. The May 14, 1858, *Minnesota Republican* reported on Anoka's effort to get rid of the town's Empire Saloon. The story began when a D. D. Dudley opened his establishment and sold "the most villainous and filthy stuff to whoever would drink it." The publication asserted that "his liquors were almost deadly poisons." Further, Dudley "succeeded, by the insidious wiles of his trade, in seducing several young men from the path of rectitude." Some wanted to force Dudley out, but a committee of seven offered to buy him out instead. Dudley's price was eleven thousand dollars for liquor and "good will." A few days later, about 1:00 a.m., Dudley woke to the sound of a battering ram breaking into the saloon door, which was secured by four locks and bolts. Before Dudley could get up, eight men rushed in, tied his hands and feet, and gagged him. They smashed fifty-five barrels and at least that many decanters and casks. The newspaper reported that liquor spilled onto the cellar floor and created a six-inch-deep flood. Guns, knives, "and such-like play-things that were found by the side of the belligerent sleeper" were tossed into the street. As the men left, one of them yanked the gag out of Dudley's mouth. "Someone whistled," Dudley said, "and I didn't see anybody any more!" He couldn't identify the intruders because they were disguised with lampblack and frizzled hair, but he knew it took them only five minutes to wipe him out. When the sun rose and Dudley looked out into the street, the first thing he saw was his wagon had been brought up to the front door and it was facing "out of town." Other liquor owners got the message their product wasn't welcome when they saw the same battering ram set up on braces in the street, aimed at their door. Notes slid under their doors warning them about visits from the "Dark-Lantern" committee sent the same message. Rumors flourished that a dozen of Anoka's most prominent citizens knew something about the Dark-Lantern committee, but they were never verified.

Another Anoka County confrontation took place at Coon Creek in October 1932. *The Anoka County Union* reported on an incident that began October 11, 1932, when fifteen trucks loaded with livestock stopped in Anoka and formed a convoy. The road they wanted to travel (in current-day Coon Rapids) was picketed by a hundred men. In light of the opposition ahead of them, the truckers agreed to wait until morning before moving out. At least, most of the truckers agreed to wait. Eleven truckers weren't as patient as the others, so they fired up their rigs and headed for St. Paul. At Coon Creek, the eleven trucks were stopped and told to turn around and head back. The picketers used red flags and lanterns and spread nail-studded belts and planks across the highway. When the trucks drove over the planks, their tires were punctured. This angered the truckers, so they jumped out of their trucks and began fist-fighting with the locals. As the fight grew larger, a woman emerged from one of the trucks and turned over all the planks so the remaining trucks could pass safely. When the picketers saw that, they ran to form a human line across the road. Anoka County Sheriff Olson and deputies arrived, and Hennepin County Sheriff Wall and his deputies arrived to find the picketers gone and the trucks stuck in place. Wall promised to keep Hennepin County roads open, and Olson promised to do the same in Anoka County. An hour and a half later, the road opened again.

Anoka County received much of its news throughout its history from the local newspapers. In 1865, George Gray of the *Monticello Statesman* became the editor and publisher of the *Anoka Union*. Gray ran both newspapers from his Monticello location. In an early issue of the Anoka newspaper, Gray printed his view of the importance of advertising to a newspaper's success.

The village of Anoka is large enough, and has enough business to fill two pages of this paper with new advertisements, and we expect to see it done. There are no papers, probably, outside of St. Paul, in this state whose subscription lists are large enough to pay for their ink, paper, and typesetting. They rely mainly on their advertising for support. We are not an exception to this general rule. Anoka wishes to have a good paper, and can have a good paper if it wishes, but cannot expect to, and never will have, a paper published for any length of time without the people advertise [*sic*]. We ought to know, and we speak the truth.

Reinforcing his point, Gray interspersed advertising *about* advertising in the body of the news column. For example, he would print, "A new advertisement of H. Knox Taylor will be found in this issue." Anoka County businesses have been advertising since business began in the county. Looking at the advertisements in old newspapers shows us a bit about society at the time. In September 1965, the *Anoka County Union* carried ads for Bob & Jane Shoes in the Coon Rapids Family Center Arcade. The store offered Poll-Parrot children's shoes in a price range of $4.99 to $7.99. Babcock Hardware in Anoka announced the September special of 4-Star stainless steel tableware. "A lovely modern pattern—gracefully shaped and beautifully polished to a lustrous satiny glow. Place setting includes knife, fork, soup spoon, and two teaspoons." The selling price? Seventy-nine cents for the five-piece setting. Then there were the bank premiums. The First National Bank in Anoka offered "Tulip-Time" stainless steel flatware (five-piece setting) free. All one had to do was bring in $25 or more and open a new account or add to an existing one. Doing so enrolled the customer in the bank's Stainless Steel Club. Each time the customer added another $25 or more, he or she could purchase another five-piece place setting for $2.50, which was a "fraction of its comparable retail value." While the advertising pricing on flatware is different between these two businesses, there was a theme going on.

From its beginning as a trading post for itinerant pioneers, Anoka emerged as a community where people settled and put down roots. In 1860, Anoka had 636 residents. Five years later, the head count had grown to 984. By 1868, more than 1,600 people counted themselves as Anokans.

In 1867, the *Anoka Union* listed fledgling county industries ranging from lumber to sash and doors; boots and shoes; furniture; plows; wagons; and brushes and brooms. There was little lacking to meet the everyday needs of the population, but the emphasis was still on the lumber industry in the 1860s. The January 2, 1868, *Anoka Union* reported, "Anoka is the headquarters of logging in the Rum River pineries. Operators living here got out last winter 13,000,000 feet of logs worth $104,000." By the late 1870s, the railroad allowed Anoka entrepreneurs to ship large quantities of their goods to customers all over the state and beyond. It was cheaper for the railroads to take the lumber already sawed by steam power in Anoka to Minneapolis than it was to have the lumber processed there. Anoka's leaders understood that lumbering was seasonal work, so they searched for diversified industries to keep people employed. By the end of 1875, the leaders' fears were coming true. There was a shortage of logs to process, and there was evidence the pine forests had limitations. Besides, too many lumber orders that had been filled on credit were unpaid, so the majority of lumber businesses suspended their credit trade. One lumber mill even filed bankruptcy, leaving town merchants with nothing but paper promises for their trust. And so began Anoka's willingness to listen to any and all enterprising ideas for industry in the city. The town was perfect in that it had ample waterpower to run manufacturing plants.

Another important part of growing business in a community is availability of financing. Three prominent leaders formed Anoka's first bank in 1874. Walter Mann, W. R. Merriam, and C. E. Blake named their establishment the Bank of Anoka, but it lasted only seven years. Reorganized in 1871, it became the First National Bank. After a few years of prosperity, the bank's cashier couldn't stand temptation any longer. He ran off with fifty thousand dollars of the bank's funds. He was eventually located in Michigan but was never brought to trial, and the money was never recovered. Instead, the bank was forced to close its doors on April 10, 1889. During the same time, another bank, the Anoka National Bank, was founded by W. D. Washburn. He enlisted the investment of fifty-seven stockholders and was chosen as the new bank's first president. With one hundred thousand dollars of authorized capital, the Anoka National Bank opened on the corner of Second and Main in Anoka on August 1, 1883. Anoka County banks have had a time of it during the county's 150 years. In 1889, like the First National Bank, the Anoka National Bank suffered a setback. There was a run on the bank, and rumors about the bank's solvency ran rampant through the community. The bank survived, however, until the Great Depression, when it failed to open its doors on January 27, 1931. In 1892, three years after the First National Bank folded, investors from Minneapolis purchased the site where it stood for sixty-five hundred dollars. Pooling another one hundred thousand dollars of authorized capital, the big city folks organized and opened the State Bank of Anoka.

Throughout history, businesses have been bought and sold, and the transaction sometimes makes the news. The July 3, 1903, *Anoka Herald* reported that J. M. Douglas & Son, furniture dealers in Anoka for thirty-four years, sold their business to R. E. Scott of Delavan, Minnesota, who purchased the store and everything in it. The newspaper said, "Monday the papers were made out that closed up a business transaction of interest to Anoka people." Then it described the many locations the Douglas furniture stores occupied—from the "corner where Hamm's saloon now is" to the second story "over A. L. Peters' drug store" to "about where the Lincoln mill now stands" to "a building on the south side of Main street at the west end of the bridge." The last location proved to be a good one because Douglas was there at the time of the 1884 fire, and he was one of the few businessmen in Anoka who did not lose everything in the fire. The report of the business sale ends with, "Mr. Scott takes hold of the business with every prospect of making a success of it. . . . He is a pleasant man and seems to have the happy faculty of making friends. . . . *The Herald* extends to Mr. Scott a hearty welcome and wishes him success."

Success came to Anoka County in many forms. One of the county's best years was 1855. People from the southern states climbed on Mississippi steamboats and headed north to St. Paul and points beyond. At first, St. Paul's citizens fretted over what to do with all the "immigrants." They didn't fret long because the people moved on and found every imaginable way to spread across the northern prairie in hopes of finding new opportunities. Joseph B. Holt opened a store at Elm Creek. Warren

Sampson opened another at Bottineau Prairie (current-day Osseo). Elder Twitchell staked his claim to land in the Grow area, and John S. McGlauflin, a blacksmith, set up his shop. Others came and claimed land. Although many didn't actually live on the land they claimed, they peppered the trees with notices to keep newcomers out. The newcomers weren't deterred, however. Instead, they continued their quest for new lives, and more of Anoka County was settled.

The rivers were low that year, so the logs couldn't get south to the St. Anthony mills. With the logs stuck in Anoka, the Anoka mill ran at capacity most of the summer. The steamer *H. M. Rice* was also stuck in the river in Anoka. The resourceful pioneers never wasted an opportunity, so they used the steamer as a temporary church and held Sunday services there until the September rains freed it up to be back in business. In early July 1855, a Red River train of three hundred oxcarts came through the Anoka area from up north. In August E. H. Davis opened Anoka's first hardware store, and Heman Ticknor opened his dry goods and grocery store. The Elm Creek and Anoka Ferry Company was organized by J. B. Holt, James W. Groat, and others. Groat built the ferryboat that made its first trip across the Mississippi on September 11, 1855. The crop harvest was wonderfully abundant, and people made good profits. Indeed, 1855 brought much success to Anoka County.

Heman Ticknor, pictured in 1865, opened one of the county's early businesses with his dry goods and grocery store.

But how fleeting is success? As fall changed to winter 1856, the people began to realize there were two sides to their prosperity coin. Although the harvest was the best ever, there wasn't enough food to meet the needs of the exploding population. Few suppliers realized how much the bulging community needed. Even fewer thought about how difficult it would be to bring in supplies with the navigation ways closed during winter. Low supply and high demand meant high prices. Salt pork brought $25 to $30 [which is about $616 today] a barrel. Corn sold for upwards of $1.50 [which is about $31 today] per bushel. Dwight Woodbury owned a new mill in St. Francis and wanted to assure his workers that they would keep eating over the winter. Woodbury went to Ball's store and approached S. C. Robbins about purchasing all the beans in the store. Because Robbins had promised provisions to other customers, he would sell Woodbury only seven bushels at $7 each. The farmers made large profits on the high prices and used the money to buy horses and machinery. New settlers watched the farmers' prosperity and bought up farmland. The increased demand for the land caused the land prices to rise. Railroads expanded and needed to buy land to lay their tracks. Since almost no one had cash to pay for all these transactions, the mortgage banking industry boomed.

It all had to end somewhere, and within a couple of years, a financial panic spread across the country. As the economic cycle goes, however, good times returned to Anoka County in 1865. The September 7, 1865, *Anoka County Union* reported, "Business at

Anoka is brisk. The water sawmill, owned by James McCann, Esq., saws about 10,000 feet per day. In one part of the mill there is a sash, door, and blind factory, employing five or six hands, and they are all kept busy." Anoka's other sawmill, a steam sawmill "farther up the river," stood near the railroad bridge. It, too, sawed 10,000 feet of lumber daily. Like the competition, it had other product lines. *The Union* reported, "The lathe machine in this mill manufactures some 7,000 per day, and the shingle machine cuts from 10,000 to 15,000 per day." On the same page, the *Union* offered this on the St. Francis sawmill: "The fine sawmill at St. Francis is sawing about 10,000 feet per lumber per day. A shingle machine at the same place cuts 15,000 shingles per day." Manufacturing also took place. *The Union* said, "A large cooperage is in operation in this town, and we understand the best kind of work can be done, although at present only four barrels are being made." Those who didn't work making barrels may have found jobs in furniture making. "D. P. Craig, Esq. has a furniture manufactory at this point, and, as we happen to know, his furniture is used extensively up river and pronounced good and durable." Flour milling had its place in the county, too. "We visited the flouring [*sic*] mill lately owned by Smiley & Woodbury—now owned by J. Mayall, Esq. This is probably the best mill above the Falls of St. Anthony and is constantly in operation."

A decade later, in 1875, residents of the county didn't know they were about to repeat the lessons of 1855. Anoka was a busy town of twenty-five hundred people. Lumber was big, and the *Anoka Union* reported, "For several years our lumbermen have been able to undersell Minneapolis in the markets of the state. It costs less to put our sawed lumber, by rail, into St. Paul and Minneapolis, than it does to float the logs down to the latter city by river—including risk of loss at the falls." Since it was cheaper to manufacture lumber products in Anoka than in the big city, the prediction by the newspaper was that new enterprises planned for late 1875 and beyond "...will, within a year, double our manufacturing capacities and more than double our population."

But as latter 1875 approached, the *Union* said, "Anoka, instead of growing and increasing in population, today is nearly at a standstill, and unless there is some manufacturing interest developed here, she will not very long remain where she is now." On August 10, 1875, the *Union* reported the bankruptcy and closure of one lumber mill. The shareholders were left with nothing. But the economic cycle continued, and in 1889, the G. H. Goodrich Company, Druggists and Stationers published a booklet to capture the imagination of anyone interested in Anoka as a community with business potential. The booklet said, "The Anoka Business College, one of Anoka's highly prized educational institutions, now entering upon the sixth year of its prosperity, ranks second to none among the commercial schools of the state. . . . Its graduates are now filling many responsible and lucrative positions." With the issue of human resources covered, the next resource a business investor needed was financial resources. The Goodrich booklet covered that, too. "Banks are run on a careful business basis . . . Anoka has two flourishing financial institutions, both of which have done their share in promoting the business prosperity." It was the time of the Wild West, which may be why Goodrich wrote, "Anoka is not and has never been what, in western parlance, is termed a 'boom' town. Its growth has been steady, but sure with no fictitious values attached."

Goodrich certainly was an expert on doing business in Anoka. Entrepreneur that he was, he realized people needed a pain reliever or ointment for their aches and pains.

He purchased the liniment formula from Mr. Hoff, the originator of Hoff's Liniment, and began making small portions of the liniment in the back of his drugstore. He offered the salve to a select group of customers, who asked for it by special request. Word spread about how good the liniment worked. Soon, Goodrich and his partner, Jennings, decided to manufacture the liniment on a grander scale. In 1889, the same year Goodrich published his booklet advising people to come and invest in Anoka, Jennings and Goodrich converted three storage rooms above the drugstore into the Hoff Liniment factory. Working diligently, they researched ways to improve the liniment. They also worked to find ways to speed up production. Since this was before the age of the assembly line, they drew upon their experiences growing up on the farm. Both had spent their youth churning butter for their mothers, so they decided to use butter churns in the manufacturing process. Sales continually increased over the years, and in the 1920s, the manufacturing operation moved to St. Paul. Goodrich died in July 1925, but Hoff's Liniment lived on until the 1970s when its manufacture ceased.

Bottles used for Hoff's German Liniment, made in Anoka by Goodrich & Jennings starting in 1889.

In 1885, about the time Hoff's Liniment made the Anoka scene, Thomas Veidt began his monument company. It remained (under one name or another) a fixture for eighty years. After Veidt's death, his two sons, George and Karl, took over the family business. The Veidt brothers were the first in the county to try the sand-blasting method of stone cutting. After they received the granite at the company, they polished it immediately. They pasted a pattern cut out of rubber on the stone. Once the pattern was securely in place, they cut it out with a spray of quartz crystals. The company featured Barrie blue granite from Vermont, as well as marble from Georgia. It specialized in the bas-relief sculpture process (the form or figure is slightly projected out from the flat surface). Eventually, the company evolved into the Anoka Granite and Marble Works. The Veidt family remained in control after the name change. The company closed in the early 1960s.

Early in the last century, another type of industry came to Anoka County. The Veerac Motor Company (Veerac is an acronym for "Valveless, Explosion Every Revolution, Air Cooled") made automobiles and even sold quite a few. Community visionaries of the New Industries Committee of the Boosters Club brought the Veerac Motor Company to Anoka by agreeing to raise twenty-five thousand dollars and using the money to buy company stock. They also agreed to give the Veerac Company five acres just north of the Reed & Sherwood factory on north Ferry Street. (Anoka–Hennepin School District offices are currently on the Reed & Sherwood location, and Schwartzman & Sons is on the Veerac location.) When building of the factory began, the *Anoka Union* reported on May 21, 1910, "The first building is to be 60 x 208 feet and is to face south with office and drafting room in the southeast corner and tool room in the southwest corner." Six weeks later, the *Union* reported the factory was almost complete. Three weeks after that, the paper reported, "A carload or more of automobile parts, including axels, brakes, etc., have arrived and a number of cars of machinery are coming. Over $8,000 worth of tools are in transit." On November 3,

1910, the factory started the first motor. On November 9, the first car was running. On November 11, 1910, that car was driven all around Anoka's streets. Folks crowded around the touring car for days until it and the second Veerac car made were shipped to New York City where they sold for nine hundred dollars each.

The automobile wasn't the only thing new in town. In June 1914, the old shoe factory building on Ferry Street closed, then reopened as the Anoka plant of the Minnesota Dry Milk Company. News of the new industry and all its promise spread. Headquartered in the Plymouth building, the Minnesota Dry Milk Company organized under the state laws of Minnesota with a one hundred-thousand-dollar investment. Quite revolutionary at the time, the dry milk process allowed the farmers a way to use skim milk that was left after the creamery and butter factories took what they needed. It also gave farmers a way to turn waste milk byproducts into money. *The Minneapolis Journal* reported, "The many excellent dairy regions remote from city markets can vaporize the milk product, reducing ten pounds of liquid to about one of dry milk that will keep indefinitely." That saved farmers shipping costs, extended selling to year round, and opened sales to world markets for top prices. The Minnesota Dry Milk Company held the patents on the basics of the process and assured the dairy industry it was not competing with, but rather working hand in hand with it to purchase what the farmers were selling. Eventually, the factory closed, but dry milk remains available today.

The old shoe factory may have closed, but the Hennicke Brothers Saddle and Shoe Shop opened at 87 West Main Street, just west of the Rum River, in 1923. Adults and children alike had their shoes resoled, restitched, or new heels put on. Almost any leather item, including saddles, could be repaired at the shop. Wanting to give a professional impression, the Hennickes kept their shop cozy and inviting. The well-oiled wooden floor boards pointed the way to the pot-bellied stove that stood in the center of the back of the shop. Customers were invited to sit and wait in the two captain's chairs that nestled near the stove. The aroma of leather and oil added to the shop's friendly atmosphere. The east wall showcased shelves of repaired shoes and other items. Huge identification tags bore a claim number that matched the one on the owner's claim check. Since this was the only way the Hennickes could identify which item belonged to which customer, they didn't release any item without a matching claim check. Customers could watch Louis Hennicke at work on his repair equipment that was set up by the wall shelves. Harvey Hennicke took over the west side of the shop with the new shoes and boots he sold. Both brothers wore leather aprons as they conducted business.

Businesses and homes in town enjoyed the convenience of electricity by 1889. But the farmers used kerosene lamps to light their homes. Anyone who has been in the county without street lamps or yard lights knows how dark the night can get. Farmers were used to the dark, but they wanted to share in the good life the way the urban folks did. Electricity was a big part of the good life. In the mid-1930s, Congress appropriated emergency funds for rural electrification. One cold day in January 1936, Anoka County farmers met at a Coon Rapids schoolhouse to

In June 1914, the old shoe factory building on Ferry Street closed, then reopened as the Anoka plant of the Minnesota Dry Milk Company. News of the new industry and all its promise spread.

determine how interested the rural community was in bringing electricity to their farms. Two weeks after that initial meeting, a group of visionaries gathered at the L. O. Jacob farm place to figure out a way to illuminate their world. They came from Anoka, Bethel, Burns, Blaine, Columbus, Fridley, Grow, Ham Lake, Linwood, Oak Grove, and St. Francis. Even though the country was trying to pull itself out of the Depression, these men believed in electricity so much that they dug deeper in their own pockets and pooled their money (all twenty-six dollars of it) to start the Anoka Electric Cooperative, now known as Connexus Energy. Once they pooled their money, the next phase was to get enough members in the community to ante up the two-dollar subscription fee so they could make a proposal for the REA (Rural Electric Association) in Washington, D.C. By December 1936, they had 469 members. Once they had the members, they needed to find a power source. Northern States Power Company (NSP) was willing to negotiate, but without any experience in working in rural areas, the going was rough. Eventually, the REA opened negotiations with NSP on behalf of AEC and several other cooperatives in the metro area. AEC and NSP signed a one-year contract in October 1937, and the rural areas had electricity ever since.

Electricity means lights, but a different Lights! Camera! Action! appeared as moviemaking in Anoka in 1949. While it wasn't the stuff of which Oscar nominations are made, it was exciting. The Federal Reserve System in Minneapolis and Reid H. Ray Film Industries Inc. in St. Paul joined forces to make a government film about the Federal Reserve story. It was slated for national distribution. Oliver S. Powell, first vice president of the Federal Reserve Bank, originated the idea and wrote the script. John Gollaudet, dubbed a Hollywood feature player in the local news, played the part of Banker Maxwell. The businessman the banker dealt with was Mr. Martin, played by New York actor Roy Walling. Martin's son was played by Robert Coleman, another New York actor. Coleman also played the love interest of a schoolmate played by New York actress Susan Thorne.

Stardom awaited some locals, too. Irma Frying, a clerk at the bank, and G. J. Hasting, the bank's president, were featured in a scene showing Frying posting checks against a customer's bank account. Doris Else of Minneapolis played the role of the banker's secretary. Carl Johnson, Anoka bank assistant cashier, shared a scene with Minneapolitans Neil Nash and Tommy McKenna. McKenna was only four years old at the time. The story line focuses on the young high school couple (Coleman and Thorne). Thorne refuses to date Coleman until he gets his schoolwork done. His assignment deals with the Federal Reserve. Anokans watched the moviemaking at the corner of Main Street and Second Avenue (the site of the First National Bank for many years). When the cameras stopped rolling, locals could see the celebrities relaxing at Carl's Café across the street from the bank. Carl's Café is long gone, but the Jackson Hotel still stands on Jackson street. It's no longer a hotel, but Billy's, a favorite Anoka eatery. Over a century after it was built for the second time, Anoka's Jackson Hotel announced it would no longer be used as a hotel. The great fire of 1884 destroyed much of downtown Anoka, including the original Jackson Hotel by the river.

The 1884 fire was the worst Anoka had seen, although the town was no stranger to fire. The first fire was February 24, 1855, when the flour mill burned. The loss was twelve thousand dollars, which made it the worst fire in the territory at that time (Minnesota wouldn't become a state until 1858). On June 18, 1856, boarders at J. R.

McFarlan's hotel barely escaped with their lives as flames shot through the halls while they slept. The smoke and people's yells rang in their minds for years afterwards. County treasurer records were consumed in the fire of May 31, 1863. As bad as the loss of records was, the loss of life was worse. People were horrified to learn a man, George C. Colbath, died in that fire. Two more fires came in 1867. On April 18, Cutters mill and tub and pail factory were wiped out. Five months later, Houston and Prescott's sash and door factory, along with Sias and Pomery's furniture factory, were destroyed. Through the night of March 13, 1869, eleven stores located in the area of Main Street and First Avenue were burned out. The loss was estimated at twenty thousand dollars. As bad as all the fires were, it got worse in 1877. On August 20, the lumberyard of W. D. Washburn and Company caught fire. More than one hundred thousand dollars worth of buildings and inventory were destroyed. Edgings had been piled up near the east bank of the river and smoldered for weeks. No sooner had the Washburn fire been extinguished than the Reed & Sherwood Lumber Yard caught fire. Damage was thirty thousand dollars. Bergsma and Company, a sash and door factory, caught fire in November. The fire raced to the old town hall and leveled it.

And yet, Anoka had not seen its worst fire. That came on August 16, 1884, and claimed eighty-five buildings—including the Lincoln Flour Mill and the Jackson Hotel—in Anoka's business section, which covered the area east of the Rum River to Third Avenue. In 1885, the Jackson was rebuilt at 217 Jackson Street, where it remains today. The new hotel boasted thirteen rooms. It was expanded in the early 1900s with a west wing that held the bar and dining room. Then the east wing was added, and the hotel grew to forty rooms. During a 1975 interview, owner Fred Jackson said, "Loggers would work a month, get paid, then come to the hotel and spend all their wages in two days. Then back they would go to work for another month." There was a time when one "could get supper, bed, and breakfast for 50 cents." The hotel's reputation for fine food brought people up the Mississippi to dine at the hotel. They made their reservations months ahead of time and often slept at the hotel before heading back down the river. Hotel employees and waitresses lived in the hotel. The dining room and kitchen closed in 1952 to make way for apartments. The kitchen was large enough to make into two apartments. Over the years, the transient lodgers were replaced with permanent residents. By 1975, one resident had lived in the hotel for forty-five years. Predictions in 1975 were that the old building with its twin cupolas, brick walls, hand-hewn oak pillars, and ornate windows would be torn down. But the Jackson Hotel still stands.

One favorite Anoka County business that no longer stands was Laws' Barbeque in Ramsey. Dan Laws owned his restaurant for thirty-five years. Born August 15, 1899, in Atlanta, Georgia, Laws left his home state when he was ten and headed north. He eventually became a cook for the Great Northern Railroad. Laws was one of the county's few African American residents, and he brought much to the county. According to his son, Kenneth, Laws worked three days, then had two days off. Instead of resting, Laws baked pies and poundcakes with butterscotch frosting, which he loaded into his car. He drove through Minneapolis neighborhoods blowing his cornet to let residents know he was there. Laws' entrepreneurial efforts weren't limited to baked goods, however. He also hunted and sold rabbits and squirrels to city dwellers. Educated through life experiences, Laws served as a deacon in a Pentecostal church in south Minneapolis and was also a champion checker player. Prior to World War II, Laws left

Bill Soderquist plowing his potato field in 1922.

the city and moved to rural Anoka County. He bought approximately three hundred acres in Ramsey, planted corn, raised chickens, and opened Laws' Barbeque in an old house that stood on the land. There was no electricity, and each room of the house had a pot-bellied stove. Customers came from all over to indulge in some of the best eating around. Besides running the business, Laws and his wife, Minnie, became foster parents to twenty-three children. In 1974, the Ramsey Lions awarded Laws its Citizenship Award, and the Ramsey Jaycees named him Man of the Year. Laws died in 1983.

Another business in rural Anoka County was Soderville's Central Garage. The Soderquist family left their home in Varmland, Sweden, and began farming in Anoka County. The Soderquists' son, Bill, rented a plot of land in Bethel and began his own farming career. Often, his farm equipment needed repairs, so Bill became a skilled welder and repairman. Word of his talent spread to his neighbors. They called on Bill to help them repair their machinery. Soderquist decided to quit farming and go into business. He purchased two acres of land at the north edge of Ham Lake where County Road 18 now crosses Highway 65. At the time Soderquist bought his land, the narrow sandy trail to it was called Central Avenue and was considered to be in the middle of nowhere. The inaccessibility to the site didn't stop Soderquist's customers from coming. They knew and appreciated his good work. His first building was a small shed. But the business grew, so in 1922 Soderquist and his brother, Gunnard, built a garage. Gunnard had trained at Dunwoody Institute in Minneapolis in automotive and gas tractor work. Since their garage was midway between Minneapolis and Cambridge, the brothers decided to name their business the "Central Garage." They used lantern light in the early days, but eventually built their own electric plant next to the garage. Within a few years the Minnesota Highway Department widened, graded, and graveled Central Avenue and turned it into Highway 65. The better road brought more traffic and customers. By 1932, the brothers built a second garage, twice the size of the first. They installed gas pumps near their new building and became dealers for Pure brand oil and gas. Over the years, the Central Garage has been more than a repair shop and gas and oil product sales. It has been a Chevrolet dealer, it has sold motor vehicle licenses, has served as an emergency first aid station and Greyhound Bus depot, and the only wrecker service between Minneapolis and Cambridge. The Soderquists came to Anoka County for a better life and ended up making life better for folks in Anoka County.

Not all businesses ended on a positive note in the county. In 1874, a man from Ohio came to Anoka with the idea of starting a cotton mill in town. Looking for financing for his project, he inquired as to how much money was available from the local folks. To show his good faith, he offered $25,000 *if* the population would put in one $100,000 by purchasing stock in the proposed mill. On November 10, 1874, the *Anoka Union* announced, "Hurrah for Anoka! The Cotton Mill a Certainty!" The article went on to say, "It is with great pleasure that we are able to announce to our readers that the Cotton Mill is now a certainty, for at a public meeting last Thursday evening, $60,500 was subscribed." The article went on to say that it understood that if Anoka raised $75,000 of the required $125,000, the Cotton Mill was a certainty. It also reported that additional stock was sold between the previous Thursday's amount of $60,500 and the day the newspaper was published, so the newspaper felt confident the Cotton Mill would be built. A couple of months later, in the February 16, 1875 edition, the *Union* relayed the bad news that little or nothing was heard about the Cotton Mill during the previous month. What was once the talk of the town became the embarrassment of the investors. The purchased stock amount stopped somewhere between $75,000 and $80,000, a bit short of the man from Ohio's $100,000 requirement. Anoka's dream of having a cotton mill vanished. No word on whether their money did the same, however.

Investment lessons weren't the only ones taught in the county. School education was an important part of Anoka County's history, too. Miss Julia Woodmansee taught classes during the winter of 1853–54 at a boardinghouse located at Second Avenue and Van Buren Street in Anoka. The next winter, Miss Sarah C. Bowen taught at the Nathan Shumway residence in Ramsey. Miss Sarah Vaughan taught summer classes at Third Avenue and Van Buren. In 1857, the area west of the Rum River was organized into a separate school district with its school near the Mississippi River. In the next few years, several other schools popped up, then closed as students went off to fight in the Civil War. After the war, the west and east districts joined and established the Irving School at Second Avenue and Monroe Street. It served students from 1866 to 1904, when it was replaced by what is now the middle section of Sandburg Middle School. The Panic of 1873 caused educators much concern. People couldn't pay their taxes, school expenses increased, and teachers weren't paid. On October 7, 1876, the school board reduced teachers' salaries, which were already low at $450 per year. The economy got better, but other issues arose. An overheated defective furnace started a fire in Washington School on November 25, 1884, at 10:20 a.m. Students were in class, but they all got out safely.

Parents in those days were as concerned about educational policies as today's parents are. In January 1885, an editorial about the extravagance of students using paper instead of slate boards for their lessons appeared in the local paper. In the 1890s, the topic was whether or not to furnish textbooks free of charge. It was years before they were provided free. In 1896, a news account about student penmanship said, "This system of vertical writing has been recently introduced and bids fair to exceed all expectations." A decade later, writing changed from straight up and down to a back slant. The back slant was short-lived, however, when the front slant we still use today became popular.

Over time, course offerings changed, too. In 1910, the Anoka High School began offering a teacher training course. A class about agriculture was added the following year. In January 1911, music was introduced in the elementary and high school curricula. Miss Carlotta was the first music teacher, and her salary was paid by Mr. and Mrs. R. W. Akin. The Philolectians provided the books and supplies needed for the students.

Anoka didn't house the only schools in the county. Crooked Lake School was built in 1859 at the north end of Crooked Lake. The school received $82.24 from the county for its first year of operation. Records from the 1860s and early 1870s are minimal, but we have better luck with the late 1870s and beyond. Early school terms lasted only two, three, or four months. Over time, however, they lengthened to seven months, divided into semesters. The winter semester started in early November and lasted four months (with one month off for Christmas). Spring semester was three months long and began in late March. Teachers often boarded with school patrons instead of having their own homes. In 1882, the school board voted to pay the teacher's board, in addition to the $125 the teacher earned in annual wages. This was a hefty raise from the $100 teachers were paid two years earlier. By 1918, teachers' wages rose to $55 per month.

Besides paying wages, the school board contracted for fuel. The school was heated with wood, which meant the wood, cut into stove lengths, had to be furnished for the entire winter and spring terms. The cost was $15 for the school year. By 1887, the cost of fuel rose to $20. Crooked Lake School got a new chimney in 1912. The next year, the state began giving state aid to the little school. As early as 1918, the school district voted on bonds for replacing the school. Since it was the time of World War I, the state asked the project be put on hold. Year after year, the little school by the lake was repaired. In 1933, the school's enrollment swelled to fifty-eight students. Since there was seating for only about thirty students, the space problem couldn't be ignored any longer. The school was moved to Ignac Holasek's farm in [current-day] Andover, and by 1938, the replacement building was completed.

It wasn't until after World War II, however, that school hot lunch came to Anoka. School cook Mabel Erickson worked at Anoka's Lincoln Elementary School (which is still located at 540 South Street). She began her career with the school district on December 10, 1949. Morris Bye, the district's superintendent, told her to prepare the first hot lunch for approximately fifty students. Since the lunch period lasted an hour and most of the students were within walking distance of their homes, few stayed in the building for lunch in those days. Not sure of what culinary delicacies to expect in the first school hot lunch, many students brought their lunch bags and boxes into the cafeteria and watched braver souls try Erickson's cooking. Morris Bye's prediction was right on, and Erickson served a little more than fifty meals. Once the students discovered they could get meat, vegetable, fruit, and milk for only twenty cents a day, the hot lunch numbers began to increase. Lincoln's principal, George Petty, began to ask the sixth-grade students to help serve the lunches because Erickson couldn't keep up with the cooking and serving all the students. Eventually, the school district hired a kitchen helper. Soon, other schools began their own hot lunch programs. For the next thirty years, Mabel Erickson served the students of the school district. She finished her career as the cook/manager of the Anoka Senior High School, where, depending on the menu, more than fifteen hundred lunches were served daily.

Service of a different kind came from county churches. Anoka's Trinity Episcopal church was formed on September 17, 1858. The faithful chose officers, legally named their congregation, and extended an invitation to Reverend Robert Paul to the first rectorship. He resigned a month later. Reverend J. S. Chamberlain accepted the position of spiritual leader, and the plans to erect a church building began. In July 1860, Bishop Henry Benjamin Whipple, first bishop in Minnesota, made the trip to Anoka and consecrated the new building. A year later, the Civil War erupted, and Chamberlain joined the military. Again, the congregation needed a leader. Undaunted, they continued their worship service without one. Finally, they found another pastor, and their future was solidified. Over many decades, the church moved, constructed new buildings, and moved again as it continued its mission.

Catholics, too, had a mission in Anoka County. St. Patrick's Catholic Church at Cedar Creek began as a mission in 1863. Except for the period 1867–71, when the church is not listed in the Catholic directories, St. Patrick's has served the people for generations. There were no Catholic directories published in 1862 and 1863. Therefore, no documentation exists to verify the popular belief that Father John McDermott, pastor of the Church of St. Anthony at St. Anthony Falls, ministered to the Catholics during that time. It is also believed he said Mass at Cedar beginning in 1863. The area was home to twenty-two Catholic families in 1857. That population alone entitled the believers to their own ecclesiastical status. We think Father McDermott was in charge of the Anoka and Cedar missions (yes, missions) until spring 1865. That's when Father Claude Genis, pastor of the Church of Saint John the Baptist at Dayton, took over the two missions. Father Lambert M. Nicolas succeeded Father Genis as pastor of Dayton and its missions in June 1866. Shortly thereafter, the decision was made to have permanent quarters for religious exercises in Anoka. Anoka's St. Stephen's Church was built, and Cedar became a mission of that church. In 1871, the plans for the Church of St. Patrick at Cedar were drawn up, and the church was built. Once a month, priests from St. Stephen's Church traveled to the new building and said Mass to more than forty area families. In 1943, St. Patrick's became the mission of St. Timothy's, a new parish in Spring Lake Park that was later reestablished in Blaine.

Faith and farming almost seem to go hand in hand—it takes a lot of faith to survive farming. One of the most storied crops in Anoka County is the potato. Publications in the late 1800s bragged that the sandy soil was better than the heavy black dirt found elsewhere because the black dirt held excessive moisture that spoiled crops. Potatoes supported many area farmers until the Colorado beetle, also known as the potato bug, appeared in 1866. Three years later, the potato crop withered to less

One of the most storied crops in Anoka County is the potato. Publications in the late 1800s bragged that the sandy soil was better than the heavy black dirt found elsewhere because the black dirt held excessive moisture that spoiled crops.

than half the size it was a decade before. Farmers resisted applying the poison Paris Green because they were fearful of poisoning the potatoes while poisoning the beetle. Gradually, their various efforts paid off, and the potato crop once again became an Anoka County mainstay. With the potato crop on the increase, a young man from Maine, Reuel L. Hall, who came to Anoka County in the 1880s, began to pursue an idea he had held for years. He dreamed of using his knowledge of extracting the starch from potatoes and setting up a starch factory in the Midwest. All he needed was financial backing, which he found in C. F. Leland, and potatoes, which he found in Anoka County. While visiting Boston and the largest starch dealer in the United States, Hall was surprised at the attitude of those in Boston who told him there was no market for his product. Despite the naysayers, Hall believed in his dream and returned to Minnesota. With twenty-five thousand dollars, he built the largest potato starch factory in the states and the first one in the West in 1886. Named Leland & Hall, the factory used potatoes planted by county farmers specifically for the starch factory. Within a short time, both the factory and the farmers made money.

By 1890, Anoka County was producing more than half a million bushels of potatoes each season. Soon, there was another potato starch factory in St. Francis and a second factory in Anoka. The factories paid good money for the less-than-desirable potatoes—those that were small or medium-sized or less than top grade. As a result of the farmers sorting their potatoes for the starch factory, they were able to send the best potatoes to the food markets and get top dollar for their high-quality potatoes. One Anoka resident, P. J. Nelson, toured Washington, D.C., in the 1920s and reported seeing some baskets of potatoes in a grocery store. The price tags read, "Fine Potatoes 75c per bushel" and "Anoka County Potatoes $1.25 per bushel."

Making potato starch began with farmers bringing their potatoes to the starch factory and getting them weighed. Once weighed, the potatoes were dumped into bins so the loose dirt could be sifted out. Then the potatoes traveled along the conveyor to the grater while a continuous stream of water washed the potatoes, getting rid of more dirt. The washed potatoes were ground to a fine pulp. Ice-cold water carried the pulp, called pumice, to a sieve where it was strained from the starch. The pumice was discarded. What remained (water and starch) got pumped into settling tanks. It took about ten to twelve hours for the settling to finish. Then the water was drained off, and fresh water was added. The tanks were stirred vigorously, and another ten to twelve hours of settling began. The process was repeated several times. After the starch was settled for the last time, the substance in the tanks was pumped to the drying floor. There it was inspected for any remaining dirt. After inspection, it was spread on tables to dry. When completely dry, the starch was put into sacks and ready to go to market to use for sizing cotton fabric. Because of its high quality, much of Anoka County's potato starch was boxed and sold for household use. To continue operation, the potato starch factory needed to produce three thousand bushels of starch every twenty-four hours. On average, a bushel of potatoes produced eight pounds of starch.

Ruth Stake started teaching in Anoka County rural schools in 1911 and recalled, "Some districts declared a potato vacation for the whole school for one, two, or three weeks. To make up this time, the term extended to May or June. This enabled boys and girls to help with the farm work in the fall and spring." In 1919, the compulsory attendance law required students attend forty days of classes. The intent was to allow students to work in the fields when necessary. Wet conditions and cool temperatures in 1938 brought on ideal conditions for a disease called Late Potato Blight. First discovered in the Anoka State Hospital farm, the blight spread quickly. Farmers began looking for other crops to plant.

World War II brought more challenges to the potato farming industry. Men went off to war, or they went to work at one of the two defense plants—one in Fridley and the other just across the county line in New Brighton. Unskilled labor made better money in the plant than they did on the farm. By 1943, a Farm Help Committee and seven work placement centers were set up in the county to help bring labor for the potato harvest out to the farm. High school kids were dismissed from class to help. Employees from companies such as Federal Cartridge helped after hours. Seventy-eight people were placed on farms that year.

One of the worst horrors Anoka County farmers faced came in the 1930s. It was the decade of the Great Depression and the dust bowl days. The grasshopper population increased exponentially because the bird and rodent populations suffered and decreased during the droughts. The dry days also destroyed the natural diseases that helped keep the grasshopper population in check. With fewer predators and diseases, the grasshopper laid more eggs, which hatched into more grasshoppers that matured into adulthood and laid more eggs that hatched and matured into more grasshoppers, and so on. An average grasshopper eats more than half its body weight in green vegetation every day. As the swarms grew so thick they darkened the sky in the daytime, they devoured a field in almost no time at all. When the grasshopper eats the leaves of a crop like corn, they kill the plant. When they eat other green vegetables right down to the ground, there is little farmers can do to save the crop. One thing Anoka County farmers tried in fighting the grasshopper plague was spreading a poison bran mash. In 1932, according to the Agricultural Service, farmers spread forty thousand pounds of poison over ten thousand acres of crop land. An estimated twenty thousand bushels of crops were saved. The biggest infestation came in 1937–38, however. Cold weather early in the 1937 growing season kept the grasshoppers from hatching. When they finally did hatch, they came out with a voracious appetite and ate corn, potatoes, vegetables, and alfalfa.

Desperate to keep from going under, the farmers formed a grasshopper control committee. An insect control officer was appointed for each township in the county. A farmer from Ham Lake, Abe Fast, took on the responsibility of mixing sawdust, bran, and sodium arsenate as bait for the grasshoppers. Within a few days, 115 tons of poison bait came out of two mixing stations. In 1938, a survey showed two to three pods of grasshopper eggs per square foot on average. Since each pod held sixty to eighty grasshopper eggs, the coming infestation looked to be the worst yet. The grasshopper control committee re-formed, began mixing poison bait, and built a spreader using a rear axle of a Model T with a fifty-gallon barrel and metal disk to help distribute the poison. After the committee showed off the first spreader at township meetings, seven more were built or bought by groups of county farmers. The mixing station saw Abe Fast as foreman over workers from the Works Progress Administration (WPA) program. To ensure all affected acreage in the county got treated, the Anoka County Board of Commissioners passed a resolution that if any property was not treated, the county would do so at the landowner's expense. Only a few localized grasshopper infestations were found in 1939. To be on the safe side, farmers spread 215 tons of bait on approximately 250 farms anyway. The grasshopper plague was over. As the grasshopper control committee worked to help farmers with problems, so did the Anoka County agent. County agencies were formed across the country after the Smith–Lever Act of 1914 was passed.

In 1915, the Anoka County Farm Bureau was chartered. The bureau had many segments. Frank Patchen headed the cooperative organization, A. L. French did live-stock improvement, V. M. Smith had soils improvement, G. Gid-

Dairy cattle on exhibit at the 1921 Anoka County Fair.

dings did the county fair, Charles Wickstrom worked on crop improvement, and L. J. Greenwald had commercial clubs. Women held leadership roles in the bureau segments, too. Mrs. W. E. Bradley had the boys' and girls' clubs, Mrs. C. W. Lenfest worked on school improvement, Mrs. Purmont did home conveniences, Mrs. Spohn did child welfare, Mrs. A. A. Boyd did clothing conservation, and Mrs. E. Eldridge had food conservation. Anoka County's first agent, Lewis O. Jacob (L. O. Jacob), held the job for eighteen years. No one replaced him until an "emergency agent," Kenneth Ingwaldson, was named in January 1934. He served six months and was replaced by C. E. Stower, who remained until 1937. From the beginning, Jacob worked with various organizations to bring solutions to problems facing county residents. He served as president of the farm bureau and as county director. After leaving his county agent job, Jacob was elected to the board of directors of the Minnesota Farm Bureau Service Company and became president of that organization in 1952. He served as their president until his death in 1959. While serving as county agent, Jacob did much to help farmers increase their farming success. Since two-thirds of Anoka County soil is sandy and the remaining third is peat, he encouraged county farmers to lime the sandy soil and plant alfalfa. To better understand the peat soil, Jacob persuaded the county commissioners to enter into an agreement with the University of Minnesota Soils Department to conduct research on the county's poor farm. The research lasted about a decade as areas of the poor farm were drained and planted in various crops. Farmers learned that fertilized peat land was perfect for growing potatoes.

Poultry offered a good income to Anoka County farmers as well. The premier poultry farm belonged to George Ghostley. Ghostley began breeding chickens in 1918. Specifically, he bred a white, single-comb leghorn. Two years later, when he married Pearl, she helped him. One of the reasons for the Ghostleys' success was trap nesting, a technique that trapped the hen as soon as she entered the nest. Since the hen couldn't leave, the Ghostleys could keep accurate laying records. If the hen didn't perform, she was culled from the flock. In 1936, the farm hatched three hundred thousand chicks and sold them in boxes of one hundred chicks per box shipped via the post office. It took nine thousand hens, eleven year-round workers, and thirty seasonal workers to keep up with the demand. The farm also grew the chicken feed needed for the poultry.

Turkeys also contributed to farming success in Anoka County. From 1940 to 1945, the county's turkey population rose from twenty thousand to one hundred thousand, while the chicken population rose from 108,500 to 155,000. World War II was going on, and the increased poultry was a result of the Food for Defense campaign from the U.S. Department of Defense. Egg prices rose, making it more profitable to raise chickens, but in 1944 there were too many eggs, and the price plummeted, making chickens less desirable to raise.

Dairy cattle always had a place in Anoka County. The Cow Testing Association was formed in 1905 and became the National Dairy Herd Improvement Association in 1927. Their work improved dairy herds and increased dairy production. By 1942, the county boasted 14,500 cows. The 1950s saw almost $1 million annually in dairy farming sales. Pressure to install bulk milk coolers, plus concern that bad springtime roads would impede big tanker dairy trucks from picking up the milk, became reasons county farmers turned away from dairy farming. Economics over the next few decades eroded the dairy farm population even more. By 1997, only 9 percent of the county's farms were dairy farms. In 2003, the county's bovine population dropped to just three hundred cows. Sixty-seven percent of Anoka County was farmed by the end of World War II. The peak year for farming was 1945, and farm acreage has decreased steadily ever since.

Moving from farmland to residential property became the going thing. One of the fastest growth spurts for residential land in the county came during the 1960s. The county's population grew 80 percent, and developers took over the farmland. Orrin Thompson, Vern Donnay, and George Butler changed the landscape forever. In 1980, Anoka County was the third most densely populated county in Minnesota. By the turn of the millennium, the county's population rose above the three hundred-thousand-resident mark.

As the county's population grew, so did its patriotism. For example, Anoka's Albert Woodbury served as a junior first lieutenant in the Second Minnesota Battery of Light Artillery during the Civil War. Woodbury was creating a comfortable life when the northern and southern states began fighting during spring 1861. His uncle, Caleb Woodbury, owned the Anoka Flour Mill, which Albert and a partner bought from him in the 1850s. Wanting to do something to help the Union cause, Albert worked at organizing a company of volunteers he hoped would become part of the First Regiment. When he discovered the First Regiment was full, he didn't give up. Instead, he sold his part of the flour mill to his brother, Charles, and joined Captain William Hotchkiss to form the Second Minnesota Battery of Light Artillery. Mustered into service during the winter of 1861–62, the Second Minnesota Battery was accepted "into service of the United States for three years, or during the war," on March 21, 1862. The battery left Fort Snelling in May. The volunteers fought against Confederate General Braxton Bragg in Perryville, Kentucky, on October 8, only six months after being activated. They also battled in Stones River, the Tullahoma campaign, Chickamauga, Chattanooga, Tunnel Hill, and Buzzard Roost before they were mustered out of service on August 16, 1865. Chickamauga, on September 18–20, 1863, was the battery's fiercest battle.

Lieutenant Woodbury served under Captain Hotchkiss. In his report about the battle of Chickamauga, Hotchkiss stated that the Second Minnesota under Woodbury's command was brought into position "under a brisk fire from the enemy's skirmishers." He further wrote, "Three successive times it prevented the enemy from forming and extending his left with the evident purpose of flanking General [Jeff C.] Davis's right." Early in the morning of September 20, the Second Minnesota was assigned a position covering the Chattanooga road. General Davis's report stated, "The Second Minnesota was rapidly brought into position a little in the rear of our line of infantry, which was soon drawn back as to give as free range as possible to the guns. My lines thus arranged . . . I was enabled to repel the repeated assaults of the enemy . . . until 4 p.m. when reinforcements arrived." Woodbury led the Second Minnesota bravely, but he paid the ultimate price. Hotchkiss wrote, "Just after the battery was got into position on the new line, a rebel sharpshooter sent a musket ball into Lieutenant Woodbury's left arm, just above the elbow, and broke the bone. From this wound he died in private hospital in Chattanooga, October 29, 1863. Thus terminated the life of an accomplished young officer, much beloved by his commander and the men of the battery." Albert Woodbury was twenty-seven years old. It is estimated that the casualties during the two and a half days of the Battle of Chickamauga were more than sixteen thousand for the Union and more than eighteen thousand for the Confederacy.

Anoka County residents served in the Korean Conflict as well [the conflict was termed a police action under the auspices of the United Nations rather than a war, largely to avoid the necessity of a congressional declaration of war]. Wayne Picket, a marine from Blaine, reported the American military lived in tents, no matter what the weather was in Korea. "I got frostbite," Picket said. "It was cold. You had two felt inserts for each shoe. We kept the spare one inside where it would dry out and changed them every day." Coon Rapids marine Ervin Lewandowski said, "We had down sleeping bags. Sometimes we'd take off our boots and set them down beside us . . . and we'd get up in the morning and [the boots] would be froze [*sic*] to the ground." Six Anoka County residents died during the Korean Conflict, which lasted four and a half years, from June 25, 1950, to January 31, 1955. There was a cease-fire on July 27, 1953, but fighting didn't end then. Thirty-three Anoka County residents gave up their lives serving in the Vietnam War. U.S. combat troops were involved from March 8, 1965, when thirty-five hundred marines arrived, until April 30, 1975, with the Communist forces gaining control of Saigon. The Vietnam War formally ended with the unconditional surrender of South Vietnam.

County defense involvement didn't always entail sending people overseas to fight, however. During the first decade of the Cold War, the Soviet Union developed a series of medium-range bomber aircraft capable of carrying a nuclear payload that could hit the U.S. The United States saw the need for a guided missile that could take down the enemy plane before it succeeded in dropping its bomb. A site just north of the Anoka–Isanti County border, called the Bethel Base, was selected as a defense missile base. It was one of our bases located approximately thirty to forty miles from the Twin Cities. The other bases were located in St. Bonafacious, Farmington, and Roberts, Wisconsin. The Bethel Base opened January 26, 1960, and consisted of two sites a half-mile apart. One site contained radar and computer systems, administrative offices, the mess hall, barracks, and recreation. The second site contained the missiles housed

The train car that carried the body of President Abraham Lincoln was lost to a 1911 fire when the Columbia Heights warehouse it was stored in burned.

in three bunkers, with each bunker having its own entrance, missile launcher, missile bay doors, and emergency escape route. The bases became obsolete, and Bethel Base closed in 1972. The administration site was remodeled as the northern branch of the Minnesota Sheriff's Boys Ranch and remains that as of this writing.

The past 150 years brought disasters of different types to Anoka County. One such event began in 1863 when the government military car shop in Alexandria, Virginia, built an extraordinary railroad car for President Abraham Lincoln and his cabinet to use on special occasions. A description of the car was printed in the April 22, 1864, edition of the Washington, D.C., newspaper, the *Daily Morning Chronicle*. It told of the parlor, sitting room, and several sleeping rooms contained in the ornate structure. While he was alive, President Lincoln used the car several times. But the car's most famous use came after Lincoln was assassinated. It carried his body and the body of his son Willie back to Springfield, Illinois, for interment. The trip encompassed twelve days, ten cities, and sixteen hundred miles. Reports were that the Lincoln Funeral Car, as it became known, traveled between two continuous lines of mourners day and night, rainy or clear. In 1866, the government ordered all its railway material sold, so the Lincoln Funeral Car was sold to T. C. Durant, one of the Union Pacific Railway's builders. He used it for several years in Colorado until it was considered no longer functional. The car was placed on display in the transportation building at the Omaha Exposition in 1898. In 1904, it was placed in a Lincoln museum built at the St. Louis, Missouri, World's Fair. After the fair was over, Thomas Lowry purchased the car in order to preserve it as an artifact and brought it to Minneapolis. He kept the funeral car in a crate with an iron fence around it in a sparsely settled area at 37th and Quincy in Columbia Heights, and thousands visited it annually. Lowry died four years after buying the car, so his family donated it to the Minnesota Federated Women's Club. Everyone expected the car to be housed at the Sibley House as part of a state museum in Mendota the coming summer, but something went wrong. On Saturday, March 18, 1911, high winds blew across the prairie. About 2:30 in the afternoon, a boy was tending a grass fire behind his house at 35th and Architect's Avenue. The winds whipped the fire out of control. Since the menfolk were working in Minneapolis, only women and boys were available to form a fire brigade. There was no water supply that far out of town. Most worried about saving the village, and few thought about the Lincoln Funeral Car parked at 37th and Quincy Street. Mrs. Henry Schoenheifer did think about it, however, and telephoned another fire station. They arrived too late; the funeral car was destroyed. Ten blocks were charred. Two boys, twelve-year-old Ian McKnight and fourteen-year-old Burdett Whitman, were burned trying to save the car, but it was reduced to charred wood, ashes, and iron. The next day, Edmond Walton, manager of the Columbia Heights Land Company, allowed the general public to visit the site and take what was left of the car as souvenirs.

A few years before the disastrous Columbia Heights fire, the northern part of Anoka County suffered a tornado. The July 3, 1903, *Anoka Herald* carried the story that began, "Old Jupiter Pluvius was busy in Anoka County yesterday." Jupiter Pluvius is an epithet (just as "the Great Communicator" was another name for President Ronald Reagan) for Jupiter, and it means rainmaker. The point is the weather must have been particularly vicious that day. *The Herald* story reported: "At St. Francis there was a very severe hail storm accompanied by strong wind. The smoke stacks of the mill and canning factory were torn down. The damage to that section of the county will be several thousand [1903] dollars." Burns fared a bit better. The story says, "Yesterday forenoon a tornado in Burns blew a number of buildings off their foundations, tumbled over sheds, and threw down windmills and large trees." The final damage report centered on Ramsey. "In Ramsey, a miniature twister descended upon the McKeen farm, occupied by Frank Rawson, where it took the roof off from a part of the house, demolished the sheds and other outbuildings, and carried a number of large trees from the front yard over into an adjoining field."

A few decades later, Anoka faced its own tornado. The Monday evening edition of the June 19, 1939, *Minneapolis Journal* carried stories told by Anoka's tornado eyewitnesses. Anoka drugstore proprietor B. J. Witte heard the storm was coming. He ran to close the store's back door. "There wasn't a breath of air in the yard," Witte said. "Overhead I saw timbers and debris floating through the air like a large school of fish. Occasionally a large plank would drift to the edge of the flow and plummet to the earth." Ernest Nyvald was the game warden who lived at Crooked Lake. He, his wife, and three children were in their car near the Anoka armory when one of the kids spotted "a long horizontal cloud gathering and whirling." Nyvald said, "I drove as fast as I could to our cottage—I made the two and a half miles in about two minutes." The storm didn't head in their direction, but they watched it do its work on Anoka. "It must have lasted about five minutes, but we could see it for ten minutes," Nyvald said. Louis Kulenkampt of Anoka was working at an oil station in Champlin near the west end of the bridge. His wife saw the menacing sky and sent him home to close the house windows. When he saw the tornado approaching from behind, he drove more than fifty miles per hour trying to outrun it, but the funnel passed

B. J. Witte and his business were lucky to survive a 1939 tornado that destroyed much of downtown Anoka.

him. Edward Morrissette was killed when the tornado wrecked his home. People searching more than a mile away from that site found his marriage license. Mr. and Mrs. Tony Manley's home was on one side of Seventh Avenue. Mr. and Mrs. H. A. Smith lived directly across the street from them. Both families ended up in their basements, but they got there in different ways. The Smiths rushed to their basement when the tornado approached. Their home was untouched. The Manleys were napping on the second floor of their home and didn't know about the storm until it burst through the outside wall and sent them plummeting to the lower level. Richard Karstedt of Champlin suffered two injuries: a broken leg and a ten-inch sliver driven through his right ear lobe. He was rushed to Eitel hospital where they removed the splinter before they set his leg. Karstedt had already missed several months of work because of a leg injury—same leg. His immediate concern wasn't so much about the prognosis for regaining full use of his leg as it was about the doctors saving the sliver as a memento for him. A car parked near Bass Lake, four miles west of Osseo, had its doors ripped off and blades of grass driven into the tires. Four people in the car died. A woman walking along an Anoka street was uninjured but lost her wedding ring when the powerful wind tore it from her finger.

When the tornado hit, there was no television or Internet. Hitler was marching across Europe. The economy wasn't doing well. And in Minnesota, the heat was stifling. Those who could went to the lake that weekend to cool off. On June 18, 1939, a Sunday afternoon, the highways were jammed with people heading back to the Twin Cities from the lake country. At 3:20 p.m., the tornado hit, and in three minutes it was over. The storm started in Hennepin County between Hamel and Corcoran. It swept past Maple Grove and into Champlin on the south side of Elm Creek. A dozen or so homes were destroyed before the storm headed across the Mississippi River to do its worst work in the heart of Anoka. Then the storm headed to the north end of Round Lake and finished its devastation just east of Coopers Corner past Cedar. Nine people lost their lives, and almost 150 were injured. A spontaneous citizen's organization, called the Citizens Relief Committee, was formed by local business and professional men.

The most damaging series of tornadoes in Minnesota slashed across Anoka County between 6:00 p.m. and 9:00 p.m. on May 6, 1965. Some sources claim two and some claim three tornadoes hit Fridley that day. But all sources agree one of the tornadoes that horrible evening was an F4 [F5 was the worst tornado possible at the time, but effective February 2007, the new enhanced F-scale is implemented]. The first tornado hit just north of Fridley Commons Park, and another one touched down several blocks south. A trailer park on the west side of Highway 65, between 73rd Avenue and Osborne Road, was hit hard. There was one fatality in the trailer park—a baby girl was killed while being given a bath.

It wasn't all disaster in the county over the past 150 years. The county enjoyed a plethora of entertainment and celebrations and sports. One of the most fun entertainers was Ruth Lee Willman Jones. Born in St. Louis, Missouri, on September 12, 1887, Ruth was orphaned at five years old. Her future looked bleak until a family friend, Mrs. Willman, adopted her. Willman had a daughter of her own and was anxious to give Ruth Lee a loving home. A well-known actress in the early 1890s, Willman trained the two girls for the stage, and they wowed the crowd as a song and dance act. The girls grew into their teens and split up. Ruth ventured west to San Francisco where she joined a stock company as an actress in melodramas and plays. She met Charles Howell

The Anoka Municipal Band, pictured here in 1935, performed during the 1939 International Pageant of Peace.

Jones, an acrobat, in Everett, Washington. She worked in one town, and he worked in another, but they still found time to keep company when they weren't performing. Eventually, they married. Following her husband's lead, Ruth became an aerialist. Their act was showcased as the Ruth Howell Duo, and they performed across the United States, Europe, and Africa. Needing a rest, the husband-and-wife team chose Crooked Lake as their vacation spot in 1922. That was the first of many vacations at the lake. In 1925 and 1926, they performed with top billing at the Anoka County Fair. As the decade of the 1930s dawned, the duo retired and settled in Anoka. Charles operated the Pure Oil filling station on the corner of Main Street and Third Avenue. After Charles died, Ruth continued to live in Anoka until her death December 15, 1950.

Another actress came to Anoka County, too. Judy Garland visited Anoka in April 1938, just one year prior to the release of *The Wizard of Oz*. Garland, a native Minnesotan born in Grand Rapids on June 10, 1922, and her mother stopped to see lifelong family friends the Hugh Logans. The Metro-Goldwyn movie star granted an interview to the *Anoka Herald* and the Anoka High School newspaper. She revealed during the interview that Spencer Tracy was her favorite movie actor and that swing music [the rage of the 1930s era] "makes people go crazy sometimes."

About a year after Garland's visit, the Works Progress Administration (WPA) assisted the *Minneapolis Journal* and the Anoka Recreation Planning Board in bringing an international peace event to Anoka. On Tuesday, July 11, 1939, the International Pageant of Peace, touted as "one of the most spectacular and colorful events ever held in Minnesota," was held in Anoka's Eastman Stadium. Theodore Veidt directed the Anoka Municipal Band in a special concert from 7:45 to 8:15 p.m. Immediately following the concert, a procession started at the picnic grounds and wound its way across the footbridge and onto the stadium. Flag bearers carried several national flags,

George Green, an Anoka businessman and civic leader, suggested the city organize a Halloween celebration in 1920.

including our own. Dutch-costumed members of the Netherlands Club led the procession of two hundred. The Russian Cossack Orchestra played Russian music while on a boat anchored in the Rum River. A Russian cast divided into two groups and surrounded the orchestra as the boat was rowed to the landing at the center of the pageant grounds. Seventy-five Norwegian males sang songs from their homeland. The Ukrainian Ballet Troupe of Minneapolis performed native dances while dressed in colorful costumes. Swedish and Danish folk dancers, dressed in authentic attire, danced as they represented those countries. An Anoka girl, dressed in red, white, and blue, was the grand finale. She stood on a pedestal surrounded by the two hundred participants, flung her arms wide open, and sang an emotional "God Bless America."

Pageants of another sort also graced Anoka County. Halloween came to America in the 1840s with the Scottish and Irish immigrants. Although clergy frowned on its celebration, Americans found upbeat ways to celebrate the dark holiday, and by the 1870s, fancy costume parties were found everywhere. As the holiday headed west, Halloween celebrants put wagons on roofs, stole gates, let cattle loose, and turned over outhouses whether they were occupied or not. In 1920, Anoka businessman and civic leader George Green suggested an organized Halloween celebration. The Anoka Commercial and Kiwanis Clubs gave him their full support, and in September a committee was formed. Soon, teachers, parents, and students joined in. Anoka became the self-declared Halloween Capital of the World. For the next month, one thousand Anoka students dreamed of their costumes. An evening parade featuring local and neighboring bands and drum corps were planned. After the parade, hundreds of bags of popcorn, candy, and peanuts were passed out to the marching costumed children. Everyone gathered at Bridge Square for a large bonfire and program. Every year the celebration grew more popular, but in 1942 and 1943 it was canceled because of World War II. By 1947, the number of marching children had almost tripled, so the parade was moved to 2:00 p.m., and all the children in kindergarten through grade three from Anoka and neighboring towns of Champlin, St. Francis, and Coon Rapids were included. The celebration has changed over time and extends beyond Halloween night, but it still is a fun community event.

Other county events involve sports. Track and field began in Anoka in the early 1880s. Community picnics and celebrations such as the Fourth of July offered both men and boys a chance to show off their athletic ability. There were the normal straight running races, but there were also some race variations we still enjoy today. Sack races (the ones where the racers hop around in gunny sacks) and three-legged races (where each of the two partners have one leg free and the other tied to their partner to form the third leg) were the most common. The winner of each age group received a cash prize.

By 1900, judges, timekeepers, regulation equipment, and an organized format brought track and field to the next level. Within a few years, the inter-class track meets evolved into heated competitions between Anoka High School freshmen, sophomores, juniors, and seniors. The meets drew excited crowds since the school served many of the surrounding communities. The 1920s saw Anoka competing in track meets outside the school, and by the 1930s Anoka's track stars were winning the majority of their meets. They did so well, in fact, that from 1932 to 1941, they won the District Track Championship every year. During their championship reign, the unstoppable team also took the Region crown in 1933, 1934, and 1937.

The 1960s saw Anoka High School's sport strength in football. A photo in a September 1965 edition of the *Anoka County Union* showed the smiling face of football coach Stan Nelson and his players standing around a large trophy, described in the caption as being forty-two inches tall. At the time of the photo, Nelson had racked up four suburban titles in twelve years of coaching at the high school. Three of those titles lined up back to back and declared the consistency of both the coaching and playing talent Anoka enjoyed in those days. The newspaper account read, "Nelson, a strong proponent of the Wing T and the Split T offenses, also boasts the longest winning streak [33] in the State, and the second longest [Jefferson City, Missouri was first] in the nation."

Football wasn't the only sport success in the 1960s. Ron Malcolm was Anoka's wrestling coach back then, and he became the fourth winning coach in twenty years. Gordie Paschka brought wrestling to Anoka High School in 1945 and stayed on one additional year to coach. Mark Klonowski returned from the military in 1947 and coached the 1947, 1948, and 1949 teams. Garth Lappin picked up the job in 1950 and stayed through 1958. Malcolm came in 1958 and, as Lappin, started his career with a state championship. State championships were as rare in wrestling as in football back then. In fact, the four coaches mentioned brought four state championships to Anoka.

A runner leaps over a hurdle in a 1940 track and field event at Goodrich Field.

Before wrestling championships, before Internet, before television, people visited each other face to face. Reporting on who visited whom, who socialized with whom, who married whom held an important position in the local newspaper. The society reporter's notebook carried names and locations of visitors, card parties, other parties, anniversary celebrations, weddings, funerals, and even reports of illness. Anybody who was anybody graced the social pages and looked for their names to make sure they were listed.

One pair who would rather they hadn't been featured so prominently in the newspaper were Anoka County sheriff candidates John Tierney and Norman McLean. They both ran for sheriff in the November 3, 1896, election. Each candidate received exactly 1,256 votes. The attorney general ruled that either candidate had the right to appeal the tie-vote decision to the district court. Seems the attorney general thought one of the candidates would take the appeal approach and, by doing so, would get a recount. If they didn't want a recount, they would get a special election. Neither candidate asked for a recount. Instead, Tierney charged that "frauds had been perpetrated" in the election. So, Minnesota's governor decided to step in and order a new election. He even scheduled a time and place to make his proclamation. However, December arrived and the governor hadn't yet made his proclamation. For some reason, the attorney general advised him against it, so the tie vote stood. During the January 1897 meeting (the first meeting of the new year), the Anoka County Board declared Tierney the winner. The appointment was almost unanimous with the commissioners voting 4–1. The lone vote did not go to McLean, who was on the election ballot, but to William Bean instead.

Given there was another contested election involving Tierney four years later, it's probably a good thing that Anoka was one of only three towns outside of Minneapolis and St. Paul that was selected to explore membership in the newly formed League of Women Voters in 1920. (The county elections *were* having some trouble.) Mrs. Maud Wood Park of Chicago was the league's national chair. She met with women at the Anoka library on April 21, 1920, to establish the league in Anoka County. Mrs. Gus Peterson, the local organizer, brought people in from surrounding townships and from each ward in Anoka. Mrs. Park spoke to the women about clean politics and a better standard of citizenship. She urged them to look at the records of the candidates as well as their campaign platforms instead of their party affiliation. It took another eighteen years before the league came to the city of Anoka. On May 18, 1938, Mrs. M. H. Spurzem held a tea for the purpose of founding a local League of Women Voters. Twenty-five attendees listened to the message and shortly thereafter organized. The League of Women Voters is still active in Anoka County.

Another women's organization in the county was the P.E.O. Sisterhood. P.E.O. works to Provide Educational Opportunities for female students. The original Chapter A was formed in Mount Pleasant, Iowa, in January 1869, by seven Wesleyan College women. Chapter Z was organized in Anoka on April 21, 1923. At that time, more than thirty thousand women were involved in P.E.O. overall. In October 1925, Chapter Z sponsored the first Girl Scouts of Anoka. Later, they turned the sponsorship over to the Philolectians but continued giving financially to Camp Pindegay. Other Chapter Z activities included book reviews, lectures, and World War II contributions (they donated 2,376 hours to the Red Cross). Working on both national and local projects, Chapter Z contributed children's books to the Anoka

Public Library, Christmas gifts for veterans' and welfare family children, baskets for shut-ins at Thanksgiving, and donations to Mercy Hospital. On April 21, 1948, Chapter Z sponsored a second chapter, Chapter CG, with thirteen members.

Some visionaries of the 1930s realized how important preserving the county's history would be for decades to come. Mrs. Lena Chase, daughter of Anoka's Dr. Giddings, called together a group of other Anoka citizens on September 15, 1934. They met in the town's library hall to consider the idea of creating a county historical society. Chase proposed the local society be a part of the larger Minnesota Historical Society and be governed by its constitution. She called the meeting to order. Dr. Scipio Bond was made chair, and Mrs. Beach McLean was named secretary. Mrs. Georgia Goss became vice president, and Mrs. Nels Barstow was selected treasurer. The constitutional prospectus allowed for three additional chairs. Chase, Arthur Caswell, and Milo Pomeroy filled those positions. Eleven signed up as the society's first members. Five others were named honorary members. Two weeks after the first meeting, the position of corresponding secretary was added to the list of officers. Mrs. Christobel Chase got the nod and began taking care of the filing and correspondence. By the next month, October, the founders had representatives from Anoka, Bethel, Burns, Centerville, Columbus, Fridley, Grow, Ham Lake, Linwood, Oak Grove, Ramsey, and St. Francis. They also signed up twenty-two additional members.

As you can tell from this book, one of the things that goes well with history is photographs. On January 18, 1949, five photo enthusiasts met with others interested in photography to form the Anoka Camera Club. They met in the cafeteria of what is now Sandburg Middle School. Phyllis Lahn was named president, Elaine Hartmann was secretary, and Marjorie Nelson became treasurer. With twenty-five charter members, the club began strong and grew stronger early on. The club held meetings at the Anoka Public Library and in the homes of its members. Eastman Kodak and Ansco Companies provided educational programs. When there were no corporate sponsors, members filled in with their knowledge. Interest in the club waned after 1950. On January 15, 1953, the last meeting was held at the Merle Day home. Only eight members braved the weather after a heavy snowstorm raged through the night before. In fairness to those who couldn't attend, another meeting was scheduled. But, as is often the case in Minnesota, another snowstorm dumped on the community, and no one was able to attend that one. Three years later, on April 19, 1956, another attempt to resurrect the camera club was scheduled. During the following two years, various camera buffs opened their homes for meetings. Finally, on January 16, 1958, the camera club was reorganized during a meeting held in the community room of Anoka City Hall.

Every community deals with crime, and so has Anoka County throughout its history. The most heinous of crimes is murder. The county's first sheriff was appointed on June 20, 1857, but there had been at least one killing in the county before that. In 1850, a man swung his paddle, and it came crashing down on the head of an Ojibway Indian, killing him. The killing was a prelude of things to come. In January 1860, two hunters refreshed themselves at a Pleasure Creek saloon. Eventually, they realized their furs were gone. They accused the saloon keeper, Michael Durgin. Convinced Durgin stole their furs, they killed him. The day after Christmas 1874,

Louis Bleau was stabbed to death at a holiday dance in Centerville. Although the motive was unknown, the killer was arrested and served prison time in Stillwater. Six months after the Christmas murder, Burns resident P. M. Daly was working in his field when a neighbor took aim, shot, and killed him. The neighbor served life in prison. As the new century dawned, an entire family was victimized in Grow. It was Sunday evening, May 27, 1900, and members of the William Wise family sat at the table when a barrage of gunfire from a Winchester rifle and a shotgun ripped through their front window. Seven-year-old Willie was killed instantly. Willie's mother, Eliza, was peppered with gunshot and suffered two days before she died. Willie's father, William, survived but was crippled by more than thirty buckshot that hit him. Willie's older brother, Joseph, age eleven, was shot in the lung and hand but survived. Miraculously, the two Wise daughters, Eliza, thirteen, and Martha, fifteen, were in another room when the shooting started. Two young men who had been "keeping company" with the two daughters were arrested, tried, and acquitted.

Little Freddie King was only nine when saloon robbers in Columbia Heights killed him in November 1904.

A different saloon story involves the issue of a proprietor being truthful about the temperance movement. One letter to the editor in the April 20, 1864, edition of the *Anoka Star*, written by someone named "Ramrod," accuses the owner of the Kimball Hotel of deception. *The Star* had previously printed, "We are informed that the Kimball Hotel has become a temperance house." Ramrod's response: "Doubtless, Sir, *you* were so informed, but *we* are informed differently. We know that the proprietors of that house are very uneasy on account of the temperance sentiment, which they have been recently reminded still exists in this community, and we know they do not feel very comfortable on account of the fines which have been imposed on them, but it is an old trick of Kimball's, whenever he fears that the vengeance of an outraged community is about to be visited upon him for selling liquor, to cause the report to be circulated that he has stopped the business." Ramrod stated Isaac Kimball had suckered people in with this deception two or three times in the preceding few months. Then Ramrod adds, "When the buzzards are gathered together, there will the carcass be found. And when the same buzzards, daily and nightly congregate at Kimball's now, as a month ago, it is fair to presume that they do so for the purpose of receiving their accustomed rations of rot gut whisky; and it can be proven, if necessary, that liquor is still sold there every day, though much more slyly than formerly."

... "We are informed that the Kimball Hotel has become a temperance house."

Although Couchman's Dry Goods store didn't sell liquor in April 1869, it was involved in a crime. While strolling a downtown Anoka street around 5:00 p.m., a citizen noticed something amiss at the dry goods store. Law enforcement officers investigated and discovered the safe blown open and the money in it removed. The proprietor say he had $360 [about $5,000 today] stashed. After a closer look around the store, the owner noticed two coats valued at a total of $40 [about $550 today], were also missing. Further investigation revealed the culprit(s) also visited Cutter's store and C. T. Woodbury's office. Nothing appeared to be missing in either of those break-ins, however. *The Anoka Police Annual Review, 120th Anniversary Issue*

(1997–98), includes the story and tells that during the week following the break-ins, Anoka's Constable Robbins and Officer Snyder "learned that one of the robbers had been arrested on suspicion . . . in LeRoy, Minnesota." Rather than wait for the Anoka police to come get him, the prisoner jumped out of the jail's second-story window. Instead of breaking a leg or arm, the prisoner broke his nose—landing head first on the ground knocked him unconscious. That was good for the LeRoy constable in charge of the prisoner because the suspect was picked up, brushed off, and taken back into the jail. Desperate, the prisoner claimed he was faint. What did the LeRoy constable do? He walked the guy to the edge of town and told him to keep walking. Then the constable turned around and headed back to the jail where he waited for Anoka's Constable Robbins. Angry at the one that got away, Robbins filed a complaint against the LeRoy constable. Then he and Snyder got some horses and "searched the county for several miles, but found no trace of their suspect."

That criminal wasn't the only one who got away. One of the most familiar confidence games in history is the shell game. Most of us have seen it if not played it. It's the game where a pea is placed under one of the three walnut half-shells; then the shells are moved quickly from place to place as we carefully watch. When the shells stop moving, we are asked which shell the pea is under. Inevitably, the one we select is wrong, even though we're sure we never took our eyes off the shell with the pea under it the entire time. The August 23, 1873, edition of the *Anoka Republican* warned of another confidence game going on in Minneapolis. It seems there were several well-dressed people, one of whom had stuck a long knife into the ground up to its hilt. The knife owner "was willing to bet" no one could pull it out with one hand. Predictably, this announcement was made just as a Swede named Smithson approached the group. The newspaper reports, "A confederate alluded to Smithson's muscle and suggested he could." Smithson believed in himself, so he "backed his faith in his muscle by proffering to wager two hundred dollars." [That's approximately $3,100 today.] Not surprisingly, the knife owner didn't have that much cash on him, so he offered to double that amount in the form of a check that he handed over to another man in his group. Likewise, Smithson handed over his two hundred dollars in cash to the same man to hold until the attempt to pull the knife was over. Smithson pulled out the knife easily. The knife owner appeared crestfallen and declared it wasn't a fair pull. His buddy, who held the check, however, declared that it was fair and handed the four hundred-dollar check to Smithson and the two hundred dollars in cash to the knife owner. Since all wagers were paid, Smithson and the group parted company. You guessed it: Smithson tried to cash the check and discovered it wasn't any good—certainly not as good as the cash the knife owner walked away with.

Cash wasn't the only thing to disappear. On Wednesday, June 15, 1892, the *Anoka Union* newspaper carried a front-page story about a disappearing woman. It seems that the Thursday before the *Union* ran the story, a passenger named Eliza Watson (or so she said) was traveling from Anaconda, Montana, to Anoka on the eastbound Northern Pacific Railroad. There was one slight problem, however. Watson didn't get off in Anoka but rode the train right through to St. Paul. The railroad attempted to make things right by providing her transportation on the next passenger train back to Anoka. Thinking all was well, the train left the St. Paul depot. Onlookers were shocked to see Eliza Watson lying on the platform crying and groaning as if in great pain. She claimed she had broken her hip, that the brakeman didn't call the station, and that she tried to get off the train after it started. She seemed to be in so much agony that several people lifted her and carried the wailing woman into the nearby restaurant owned by Mr. Wiley. Dr. T. J. Reid, the railroad physician, hurried to the restaurant where he examined Watson. He did not find anything wrong with her hip, but he did find a bottle of whiskey she had hidden. A few minutes later, Watson and Mrs. Wiley had words, and an angry Watson stood up and marched out of the restaurant back to the depot. Curious about what Watson would do next, people watched her. The more they watched, the more obnoxious she became. Railroad agent Ogsbury was brought in on the case, but when he arrived at the place Watson had been, she was gone. No trains had come and gone, so she didn't leave by train. No one saw her leave by any other method. It was truly a case of the disappearing woman.

An anonymous person telephoned Mr. M. J. Boucher in 1904 and told him his son, George, had been shot in Bemidji. That was the entire message. Desperate to find out if his son was dead or live, Boucher called on the *Anoka County Union* for help. The newspaper account read, "The *Union* took the pains to inquire from the *Bemidji Pioneer*, and in a letter that paper says that no such accident has occurred in Bemidji, and no one is suffering from a gun wound in the hospital. That no one is in the Crookston hospital either, and it looks very much like a fake." The story seemed possible to the father since the younger Boucher worked in the Bemidji area all winter. Boucher knew his son left for Bemidji. He knew he had received an anonymous telephone call telling him his son had been shot and there were no gunshot victims in the local hospitals. But he didn't know about his son's fate until his son finally sent him a letter of explanation. It seems the younger Boucher was shot in the leg. However, the bullet didn't strike the bone, so instead of going to the hospital, he went to a friend's house to recover. The mystery of the gunshot was solved, but no one ever discovered who placed the phone call in the first place.

Another mystery occurred in 1913 when a customer got a shave and haircut from H. B. Hutchins in Anoka. After his grooming, the customer asked if he could rest in the basement for a while. Seeing no harm in that, Hutchins agreed. The clock struck 6, and it was time for Hutchins to lock up. He called down and asked the customer to leave. The customer refused. Hutchins had noticed the customer had a gun but thought little of it at the time. Once the man refused to leave, Hutchins sent for Police Chief Haley. There was a prop in front of the basement door that Chief Haley had to reach down to remove. Big mistake. The man shot his .32 caliber revolver upward, and the bullet penetrated Haley's scalp over the right eye. The bullet continued toward the back of Haley's head and exited near the top. Bleeding but still alive, Haley started to go after the shooter. Hutchins had the presence of mind to grab Haley and pull him back. Then Haley sent for Sheriff John Casey and Casey called Fire Chief George Frauman. Frauman laid two lines of fire hose to the basement, and Fred Merrill placed the fire nozzles right by the basement window. The shooter fired at Merrill but missed. Soon, there were armed men stationed all around the barbershop. Haley tried to enter the basement, and once again the man shot at him. Haley fired six shots in return. Eventually, the waterworks plant put on the pressure. The drugstore owners supplied a vial of oil of mustard and bottles of 30 percent ammonia. All of these were put into the basement. Still the man refused to leave. Someone broke down the door, and the man stood with a piece of well pump ready to kill whoever came in. It ended when one of the men saw an opportunity to grab and overpower the man. He was taken to jail, where he said if he had more guns, he would have gotten some of the crowd. Haley had his wound dressed, and he returned to work the next day.

Another criminal who didn't get away was a robber in November 1919. Roy Willis was on his way home from a dance about 1:00 a.m. when four men accosted him. He was walking outside the building that housed the Constance post office and store. "Get the storekeeper," one of them growled. "We ran out of gas." Willis knew where A. E. Halvorsen, the store owner, lived, so he went off to get him. When Halvorsen arrived, the four men drew their pistols and pointed them at Halvorsen. They told him to open the store, then pushed him in through the doorway. When the robbers demanded the combination to the safe, Halvorsen told them it was a new combination and he didn't know it. Frustrated, the men settled for stealing $200 [about $2,400 today] in postage stamps instead. Then they ordered Halvorsen to drive them to Minneapolis in his personal car. Imagine their surprise when Halvorsen's car broke down on the way. They fled without realizing Halvorsen had a strong box in the car with $750 [$9,200 today] in it. In the meantime, the Minneapolis police caught up with the robbers. The police and robbers exchanged gunfire, but the criminals got away. As is often the case, one of the men committed another robbery. This one took place in St. Paul in December. After his arrest, he confessed to participating in the Constance job.

We've looked at the settlers, their ethnic backgrounds, and a little about the communities they built. Then we glimpsed the transportation they used to move from place to place.

The people built their communities with law enforcement officers, firefighters, post offices, businesses, schools, churches, and organizations. They worked the land and defended it in wars. They celebrated life, holidays, and each other. They also suffered calamities—some brought on by man's weakness for drink or greed or crime and others brought on by nature.

The Anoka County Historical Society brought together the photos in this book so you can see life in the eyes of those who came before. May you enjoy reading and viewing *Picturing Anoka County* as much as we enjoyed bringing it to you.

1

On the Road:

Anoka County Transportation

As people moved into Anoka County, the need for transportation became readily apparent. Over the past 150 years, almost every form of transportation imaginable has found a home in Anoka County.

Nature's interstate, the river system, offered transportation on both the Rum and Mississippi Rivers. As you browse this chapter, you'll see a cook boat that followed the logging crews around. You'll also see the result of Anoka County ingenuity in the form of bridges across the Mississippi River in Coon Creek and the Rum River in Anoka and Oak Grove.

The Rum River offered more than a route to travel or obstacle to cross. It also offered swimming fun north of Anoka around Seventh Avenue, where the Rum delineates Andover from Ramsey.

But not everyone relied on the waterways to get around. Banfill-Locke in Fridley was a stopover point for those using the Red River Trail. Oxen pulled noisy, squeaky oxcarts along that trail; however, another majestic animal, the horse, proved to have more staying power as far as transportation went.

Horses pulled sleighs so farmers could get around in the winter. They also pulled trucks out of the mud, and road construction equipment that was used to build and grade the roads to keep the trucks from getting stuck in the first place. Horses needed a place to stay at the end of the day, and Anoka city stables on Third Avenue filled that need.

Bicycles filled the need for those who couldn't keep a horse but wanted to get around faster than walking allowed.

Although streets were built primarily to allow for easy passage from point A to B, they also came in handy for lining businesses along either side of the street, as you will notice in the picture of Bethel and the railroad station there.

Some people liked to ride rather than drive, so they took the train, the streetcar, the bus, or the plane. Mass transportation has been around a long time. Back in 1885, horse-drawn streetcars carried people from Anoka to Minneapolis and back on regular routes. Gasoline, then electricity replaced the horses.

Once they came to the county, gasoline transports seemed to take over every transportation form. Anoka's Main Motors started in 1919 and is still going. Buses ran from Anoka to Minneapolis in the 1940s and are still going. Airplanes took off and landed using three different county airports, and the Blaine airport is still going.

Earlier, I mentioned nature's interstate of rivers. Well, man made an interstate, too, cutting through the county at Lexington and Circle Pines. We call it I-35W.

Looking over the past 150 years, it's evident Anoka County enjoyed almost every type of transportation possible. Some forms come, some go, but throughout history the county keeps moving.

Above: *Banfill Tavern in Fridley, 1997. Built in 1847, the tavern was a well- known stop for settlers traveling along the famed Red River Trail. Set in Manomin (now Fridley), it sat on what is known as the Metropolitan Trail as it passed through innkeeper John Banfill's property. In 1851, Banfill added a store and post office to the Greek Revival building. The site, added to the National Register of Historic Places in 1976, now serves as the home of the Banfill–Locke Center for the Arts.*

Right: *Logging was a labor-intensive industry, and feeding the men was essential. This is a cook boat that followed the crews around to provide them with meals. It is pictured on the Mississippi River, but its exact location is unknown. The photo is dated 1880.*

Top left and right: *Wooden ribbing for a dam's draft tubes, 1913. Workers installing a turbine inside the powerhouse, 1914.* **Bottom:** *Construction of the spillways, 1913.*

The first mention of building a dam on the Mississippi River in Anoka County was in 1898 when the Anoka Herald *reported that the Twin City Transit Company was considering such a project. At the time, they preferred a location in Fridley, near Rice Creek, but the landowners rejected the sale. Eventually, the Dunn family, who owned much of the land near Coon Creek, agreed to sell 169 acres in 1909. After further delays, construction finally began in December 1912.*

Within weeks, a small village for the workers and their families was constructed on the banks of the river. With more than one thousand men employed on the project (three-quarters of them Anoka County residents), the town had all the amenities present of any other town of its day. It consisted of bunk-houses for the men, some private homes, cookhouses, a paymaster's office, a blacksmith shop, a school for workers' children, a hospital, and a jail. It even had a police force and a sewer system.

Construction of the dam, which spanned 2,150 feet from bank to bank, included forty-two thousand cubic feet of concrete and made use of eight hundred train car loads of crushed rock. By 1966, the dam, which generated power for the Hennepin County side of the river, was no longer able to meet the power demands for the region and ceased production of electricity. Today it operates as a park in a partnership between the Three Rivers Park District and the Anoka County Department of Parks and Recreation.

Left top and bottom: *In spring 1912, high water damaged the Pillsbury Mill dam on the Rum River in Anoka, causing portions to wash away. The dam was patched until repairs could begin in August. The entire bulkhead of the dam was removed and rebuilt with concrete and steel. The repairs took three months to complete.*

Below: *A floodgate in the Rum River dam in Anoka during winter 1975.*

Top: *Minnesota winters are no time to pull wagons, so farmers used sleighs to get around. Pictured here is the Warren Allerton family of St. Francis.*

Bottom: *S. J. Johnson knew how to make his horses look their best at the city stables on Third Avenue in Anoka. The animals' tails are braided and bowed for a portrait of the north ends of these southbound horses. The caption in the photograph notes that S. J. Johnson was a "deler in fine horses."*

Left: *It's hard to imagine the tiny community of Bethel (pictured here ca. 1910) as being one of the bustling towns in the county, but it was a railroad stop in the early 1900s and a thriving community. This downtown scene shows a group of citizens gathered near the land office headquarters, the furniture store, the drugstore, and a millinery shop. Undated.*

Below: *The W. M. Bean Bicycles and Sundries store in Anoka ca. 1909. Note the wooden sidewalks in front of William Bean's store and the styles of bikes he was selling. Do the handlebars of the bike on the left look like something from the 1970s ten-speed era? These early bikes probably had inflatable tires (called pneumatic) and a single-speed chain drive. The Beans were among the early settlers in the Anoka area; William's father, Martin, came to work in the lumbering industry in Anoka County in 1855. After serving in the Civil War, he opened a hardware store in Anoka in partnership with C. S. Guderian. Martin eventually bought out the partnership and continued in the business with his son, William, pictured here. Martin died in 1915 and William in 1925.*

Top: *Main Motors on Main Street in Anoka ca. 1925. The Carlson family opened it in 1919 and sold automobiles to an increasingly mobile community. It has had more than one location on Main Street in Anoka but still thrives to this day.*

Bottom: *Cities Service Gas Station, owned by George B. Morrill, pictured in 1943, sat at the corner of Seventh and Main in Anoka. George's father, George W. Morrill, came to Anoka in 1873 to practice law. George W. was twice elected to the office of Anoka County attorney.*

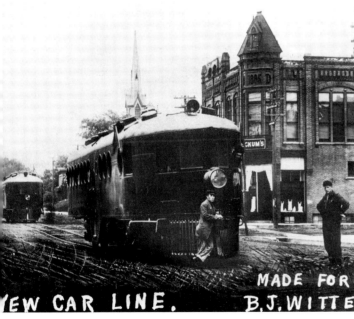

Streetcars and mass transit are not new to Anoka. The first streetcars to carry passengers were horse-drawn and transported people to Minneapolis along Ferry Street and back, with regular routes as early as 1885. The gasoline-powered streetcars replaced the horses in 1913 and paved the way for the next generation of streetcars, those powered by electricity in 1916. The last streetcars left the tracks as personal automobiles began to appear. The streetcar tracks were pulled up for the metal rails in 1939.

Above: *A scene from a road construction project sometime in the early 1920s. Charles Weaver came to Anoka County in the earliest years of the 1900s and set to work making a life and a legacy. He became one of the larger contractors in the state, as he and his crews built many roads throughout not only Minnesota but the nation.*

Top left: *This dining hall, located at the Weaver family home on Rice Street, fed workers who operated the horse-drawn equipment on the construction projects. Weaver family descendants remain in Anoka County yet today and continue to be an active force in its development and growth.*

Middle left: *Before pavement covered the streets and roads of Anoka County, wet weather and heavy usage made the roads rutted and difficult to travel. Harry Bergerson is grading the roads with a horse-drawn road grader. The photo is undated but probably was taken in the 1910s or 1920s.*

Bottom left: *A team of horses was needed to pull out a truck stuck in the mud along the county line in East Bethel in the early years of the twentieth century.*

Left: *Seen behind these county and city officials is a map proposing ramps and interchanges on what would become I-35W as it passes through the southeast corner of Anoka County. The interstate highway system, which began to bring freeways to Anoka County in the 1960s, was created under President Dwight D. Eisenhower as a means of defense and evacuation in the event of an emergency. Freeways linked major downtown areas throughout the nation, but it also made it much easier to commute to work in the city from a suburban home. This soon became known as "urban sprawl," and Anoka County, being on the edge of the Minneapolis/St. Paul metro area and linked by freeways, was not immune. The freeways in the county in 2007 are 694, 35-W, 35-E, 610, and portions of 10, all concentrated in the southern part of the county.*

Right: *This crossing of the Rum River, known as the Gillespie Bridge, was in Oak Grove on County Road 22 (also known as Viking Boulevard). The old bridge was replaced in 1962.*

Bottom right: *Construction of the Highway 610 bridge over the Mississippi River, 1986. Work began in 1986 after more than a decade of planning and public input. The project is slated for conclusion in 2007. Cenaiko Lake, part of the Coon Rapids Dam Regional Park, was formed by the excavation of soil for the highway.*

Below: *A favorite place to swim in the Rum River was where 7th Avenue (also known as County Road 7) crosses it between Andover and Ramsey. The river was relatively shallow there, and the current was not too strong. For many years, county children dared each other to get an extra thrill by jumping from the bridge into the water below. This photo was taken in 1975. The bridge was known as the Faherty Bridge and was replaced with a wider, modern one in the 1980s.*

Top: *"The whistle of the engine is now heard in Anoka!,"* the Anoka Union *headline proclaimed on December 12, 1863, and transportation between Minneapolis and Anoka became faster and easier. A line from St. Paul to Duluth served the eastern side of the county, and the Coon Creek cutoff brought the tracks through the heart of the county in 1899. In the early 1960s, these tracks were still following the same route by trains, when Amtrak began a Twin Cities-to-Duluth run. The dedication of the Cedar Crossing brought these dignitaries, left to right: Mr. and Mrs. John Nordin, State Representative Gene Voss, Bill Nelson, County Commissioner Bob Burman, unknown state trooper, and County Commissioner Ed Fields.*

Middle left: *The Anoka–Minneapolis Bus Company provided regular service for riders in the 1940s with a stop on Main Street in downtown Anoka.*

Middle right: *Changes in the Minneapolis–St. Paul area saw the implementation of a Metropolitan Transit Commission. This bus was a part of that system to take passengers throughout the metro area, 1985.*

Bottom: *A "bus service on demand" enterprise came into being in Anoka County in 1991 with the start of the Traveler. Citizens could arrange to be picked up at their doors at specified times and taken to their destinations within the county. By 2005 the Traveler had regular routes within the county as well as door-to-door service.*

Top: *Air travel in the county began in 1927 with an airstrip owned by Ted Hanson, Anoka County sheriff. who was its main user. He sold the strip, located just outside the eastern limits of the city of Anoka, to George Pierce, and it became known as the Pierce Airport. Soon, hangars were built, and many began using the facility. After WWII, the Pierce Airport took on an "air park" theme, with people building their homes nearby and keeping their planes on their property. The Pierce Air Park in Coon Rapids was one of the first in the nation when it began in 1954.*

Two more airports opened in the county—in Ramsey and Blaine. Ramsey's airport was known as the Gateway North Industrial Airport and began in 1972. It was intended for use by corporate and industrial park planes. By the 1980s, the airport needed to expand to survive, but a referendum to allow the city to buy the airport and expand it failed, and it closed in 1991.

Janes Field in Blaine was built by the Metropolitan Airports Commission in 1952 and, in large part, was to support the University of Minnesota flight programs. It was named for Phillip H. Janes, a longtime FAA employee in the Twin Cities metro area, and has paved runways and supports small jet aircraft as well as many vintage and restored airplanes.

Bottom: *A 1932 tornado that struck this airplane left a great deal of damage to the field owned by H. T. Hanson, a county deputy sheriff.*

2
Serving the Community:
Anoka County Public Services

One of Anoka County's best attributes is its communities. Much of the county's history is documented in the county seat's newspapers; thus, we are heavy in history in and around Anoka. But that doesn't mean communities throughout the county neglected to serve their people, as you will see when you look at this chapter's photos.

The county's business is conducted in the courthouse, but the county board of commissioners and the county auditor reached out to the people by making appearances and offering glimpses into their workplace.

The county sheriff, too, showed a well-rounded workday, sometimes dealing with criminals and other times preparing to deal with the pressures of the job.

Communities felt safe with their own police and fire departments as well. Circle Pines, Spring Lake Park, Centennial Lakes, and Anoka all stood at the ready for any emergency or need their communities had.

Sometimes emergencies were medical, and Anoka County shows a strong history of caring for those in need of medical attention. Anoka alone boasted the Kline Sanitarium, Mork Hospital, and the North Metro Regional Treatment Center and several private facilities. Fridley offers Unity Hospital, while Coon Rapids is home to Mercy Hospital.

While it's good to feel safe and secure, it's also important to reach out between communities and beyond. County communities had post offices, telegraph, and telephone communication channels to ensure residents could send and receive news.

Of course, utilities meant a lot to quality of life, too, especially in the early days when the county was more rural than suburban. The Rural Electric Association (REA) did a lot to modernize the county.

The more people talked, the more they learned. The more they learned, the more they wanted to know. That's where the libraries came in. Many community residents spent hours at the Anoka Carnegie Library. Eventually, the Anoka city library joined the Anoka County Library system. Columbia Heights remains the only city library in the county.

As more people moved to Anoka County, various communities met the challenge of supporting all the new homes and businesses by expanding city services to include water, sewer, and gas. Spring Lake Park even turned its water tower into a work of art to celebrate the country's Bicentennial.

Communities ran scrap drives to support the country during World War II. Today we extend the idea and call it recycling.

A glance at the pictures of the county communities over the past 150 years shows Anoka County offers a good track record in meeting its citizens' needs.

Top left and right: *Anoka County's first official courthouse was built in Anoka in 1878 on the block bounded by Main and Jackson Streets between Third and Fourth Avenues. It served well as the seat of county government until the rapid growth of the county's population following WWII. It was replaced in 1960.*

Middle: *The Anoka County Board of Commissioners and the Anoka County auditor visited plots of reed canary grass at Coon Creek on October 7, 1933. Left to right: Henry Nutter, Chris Ramsden, William Ringband, August Peterson, E. A. Carlson, and George Sanderson.*

Bottom: *Life in the Anoka County Sheriff's Department did not include shootouts or raids every day. It was the daily custom to have a game of rummy to pass the time between calls. This game was held in the office of Sheriff Red Pratt. His office was on the north side of the Trail Inn at the southwest corner of Main and Ferry Streets in Anoka. Left to right: Emil Swanson, Bill Miller, Walter Bowers, Red Pratt, Harry Gehr, Laurence Brown, and William Wuest.*

Right: *In August 1954, a formal ground-breaking was held to launch construction of a new courthouse. The men pictured at the ceremony are: Commissioner Henry Stack, Commissioner Fred Knodt, an unidentified man, and Commissioner Gus Johnson. Behind Johnson is County Highway Engineer Everett Vevea. The remainder are unidentified, including the photographer who is trying to get an official photograph.*

Below: *The new courthouse was completed and the old courthouse razed in 1960. This view shows both buildings side by side on the block.*

Left: *The 2006 Anoka County Board of Commissioners: left to right, Dick Lang (District 2), Dennis Berg (District 1), Rhonda Sivarajah (District 6), Chair Margaret Langfeld (District 3), Scott LeDoux (District 5), Jim Kordiak (District 4), and Dan Erhart (District 7). These elected officials, responsible for establishing county policy and providing oversight to the county's budget, were instrumental in the celebration of Anoka County's 150th anniversary. Their leadership in the formation of the Sesquicentennial Executive Board and the county's financial commitment were vital.*

Left middle: *A peek inside the county auditor's office in the Anoka County Courthouse in 1925–26. Note the electric lights hanging from a cord in the ceiling, and the typewriters. This particular image was made from a glass slide and was shown to audiences waiting for the movies to begin at the theater in Anoka.*

Left bottom: *The Anoka County Sheriff Department's ranger unit in 1980 with the variety of equipment they used in keeping residents safe.*

Right: *Before programs such as Social Security, Anoka County had a "poor farm" for people with no means. The county owned the farm and provided overseers or caretakers, and the residents worked the farm in exchange for their room and board. The Anoka County Poor Farm was located on what in 2007 would be the athletic fields for Coon Rapids High School on Northdale Boulevard. The Coon Rapids Historical Commission placed a marker near the site.*

Below: *Anoka County's Sheriff Uriah Pratt, better known as Red Pratt, led a raid on a moonshining operation in summer 1927. They confiscated this equipment used in the making of illegal liquor. From left to right: Fred Flath, Sheriff Red Pratt, Arthur Smith, Deputy H. T. Hanson, Special Deputy Jim Caldwell, Deputy Jacob Heller, Chester Coulter (seated), and Artie Ward.*

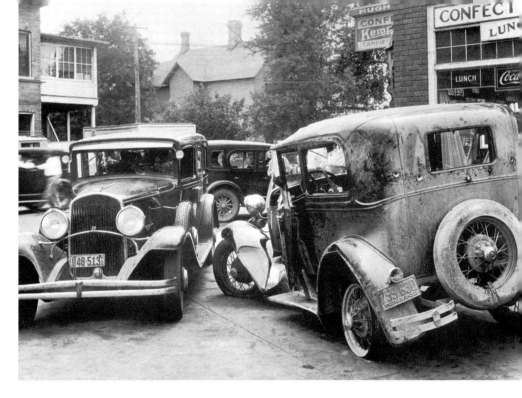

June 8, 1930, saw Anoka County Sheriff Red Pratt and his men in a wild shootout and car chase worthy of a scene on TV. The Model A Ford on the right was driven by two bank robbers. The Sheriff's Department was asked to assist by setting up a roadblock as the men passed through Anoka. The robbers escaped by driving over the curb at the intersection of Main and Ferry Streets in Anoka and heading over the Mississippi River bridge. Deputy Sheriff H. T. Hanson and Pratt had a running gun battle with the thieves in which the thieves shot out the windshield of the sheriff's car. Hanson shot back through the now open windshield and hit the driver of the getaway car near the Earl Brown Farm on Osseo Road.

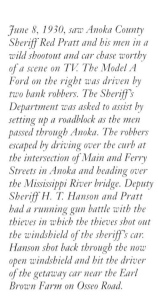

Above left: *The Circle Pines Police Department in 1968 stopped for a coffee break with a local resident.*

Above: *Centerville, Circle Pines, and Lexington are among the smaller communities of Anoka County, so working together to provide for the citizens has been a common practice. Their police department is known as Centennial Lakes, combining their school name and a geographical feature found in or near each community.*

Left: *The Spring Lake Police Department began in 1954 with two constables who worked part time and were called at their homes by mobile telephone. The department came under civil service in 1965, and by 1966 there was a full-time chief and five employees. When the department didn't have a chief, the mayor filled in. Seen here is Chief Otto Lind by his squad car in front of the Spring Lake Park Police Department about 1967.*

Shown below are the Lexington Police Department's first full-time officer and volunteers in 1960 and the Lexington squad car in 1972. **Right:** *The first Lexington police officer was Joseph Matzke, a part-time volunteer, in 1954. A volunteer part-time chief soon joined him, and they were paid $10 a month. The first police car was bought in the early 1950s, doubling as the ambulance. In 1956 the volunteer force was replaced with a paid force consisting of eight part-time officers who were paid $20 a month. It was not until 1960 that the first full-time officer was hired for Lexington. In 1973 a joint agreement between Lexington and Circle Pines combined their efforts. When the new combined department began operation in 1976, three officers shared a 1973 police car from the old Lexington department that got "six miles to the gallon and two to four quarts of oil to the eight-hour shift," said the new police chief. Another merger of departments came in 1991 when Centerville joined Lexington and Circle Pines. Today this joint force is known as the Centennial Lakes Police Department.*

Top: *The Anoka City Fire Department operated from the lower level of the old city hall that stood on the north side of Main Street between Second and Third Avenues. On display are two pieces of its equipment in 1928. The sign on the building above the trucks—"Public Restroom"— denotes the first such facilities in the city, which were made possible by the efforts of a women's organization in the city.*

Above left: *In addition to fighting fires, the Circle Pines fire department members helped celebrate the community with "Casino Night" (three men are setting up a table) in February 1967 and were top contenders in waterball games—competitions where teams with fire hoses push a large ball on a cable toward each other.* **Right:** *The kids were welcomed in to see the department's new truck on October 8, 1964.*

Left: *Fire protection has been needed in the county since the earliest days when fires were capable of destroying a whole community in a single night. A prairie fire wiped out the budding community of Glen Cary in Ham Lake in 1857 to the point where most of the settlers lost everything and moved away. A huge fire in August 1884 gutted Anoka's downtown area, forcing the idea of more fireproof buildings and a rapid rise in popularity of bricks from the county's brick-manufacturing companies in present-day Andover and Coon Rapids.*

1951 Fire Department Fleet

Top: *The Spring Lake Park Fire Department in 1951, two years before the village of Spring Lake Park was incorporated. The community of Spring Lake Park was first known as a neighborhood within the township of Fridley. As it was developed, the citizens banded together to improve their community. They worked to get the roads graded, speed limits imposed, cleaned up Laddie Lake, and organized fire protection.*

Bottom: *After spending all night fighting a huge grass fire along Lake Drive in 1949, Circle Pines residents began to think about having their own fire department. They voted to create one in 1950 with a borrowed tow truck that carried two fifty-five-gallon drums of water and a couple of pumps. Later that year, they purchased a 1929 Model A fire truck for $795. By 1955, the department members had built a tanker truck, and voters approved the building of a fire barn. It would hold four vehicles, a fire office, and a city office. More growth in the 1980s led to the development of a three-community fire department called the Centennial Fire Department. It encompasses the cities of Circle Pines, Lino Lakes, and Centerville.*

Left: *Unity Hospital was built in 1966 on Osborn Road in Fridley after years of planning and construction. It was a project by the North Suburban Hospital District and financed by revenue bonds. The project did have a setback most hospital construction projects never face—the site suffered serious damage from an F-4 tornado on May 7, 1965. Despite the damage, the building was completed on time and the first patient admitted on May 23, 1966. This photo was taken in the 1970s.*

Below: *This facility has gone through a variety of names from its beginning as the Insane Asylum in 1899. For many years, it was known as the Anoka State Hospital and charged with the care of those unable to take care of themselves. The most recent name change, North Metro Regional Treatment Center, reflects a changed mission in a modern facility, though it is still located on Seventh Avenue North in Anoka. It no longer focuses its care totally on the mentally handicapped.*

Top: *Mercy Hospital construction began in 1962 and was completed in 1963. One baby was born there during a snowstorm even before the hospital opened. Appropriately, her parents named her Merci. The hospital is located at 4050 Coon Rapids Boulevard. The addition shown here was added to the Mercy Hospital complex in 1972–73.*

Middle: *Dr. James Gates had rooms in his home on Ferry Street in Anoka that he used for hospital rooms. Many area babies were born in this hospital, as it was one of the few hospitals in the county. By the 1940s, this facility was called the Mork Hospital for the doctor who was working there, Dr. Frank Mork.*

Bottom: *Dr. James Kline ran the Kline Sanitarium at the southernmost end of Ferry Street in Anoka. He is shown here with his family ca. 1915–20.*

Top: *The first mail cart route for Anoka County brought mail to people's homes in the rural areas. J. W. Clark was the postmaster at the time.*

Bottom left: *Mort Post Office was located in the Purmort household in Bethel from 1897 to 1904.*

Bottom right: *Ellen Madsen Larson (pictured) helped out during the Christmas rush and stayed on for many years at the Circle Pines Post Office. The first facility was in the local café when it began in 1949. The mail was brought in, left on a table, and residents came to pick up their mail, a part of the cooperative community plan. V. S. Peterson was the first postmaster.*

Top left: *A worker at the Circle Pines branch library was busy putting books on the shelves in March 1978, with an opening planned later that year. The Anoka County Library system began with a study in 1956 outlining the status and projected need for library services in the county. At the time, only two libraries existed in the county—Anoka and Columbia Heights. The study, ordered by the County Board of Commissioners, provided several plans that would bring library services to all the people. The present system of libraries operating throughout the county in cooperation with the city libraries grew out of that plan.*

Top right: *The Columbia Heights City Library, founded in 1928, was housed in the Heights Theatre building on 40th and Central Avenue in 1933. Harriet Blythe, president of the Silver Lake School Mothers' Club, presented the idea of a public library in Heights. With less than $100 to purchase materials, members of the Mothers' Club canvassed on foot with children's wagons soliciting donations of books and magazines to start the library collection. Today it is the last remaining city library in the county, as all other city libraries have merged with the Anoka County Library.*

Bottom: *Community efforts and matching grant money provided funds for the construction of Anoka's Carnegie Library in 1904. The Philolectians, a women's organization devoted to the love of learning, were instrumental in organizing the efforts to raise money for its construction. Founded in 1890, the organization still thrives today with an extensive and active membership. The loss of the building, which was razed in 1965, is still lamented by many citizens of the area.*

Top and middle left: *On January 3, 1936, a meeting for all farmers in the county was held in the Coon Rapids Schoolhouse. The purpose was to gauge interest in organizing a rural electrification program. Within two weeks, $26 was raised, and an annual subscription rate of $2 was established. A successful application was sent to the Federal Rural Electrification Administration, and the first electrical line ran in the Crooked Lake area. To celebrate the occasion, 311 people turned out at Mrs. C. J. Sorenson's resort to witness the first electric lights turned on March 23, 1938. Eventually, the co-op took the name Anoka Electric Cooperative and today is known as Connexus Energy.*

The Anoka Electric Cooperative, shown in the top photo in 1980, held demonstrations (middle photo) throughout the community, including at the Anoka County Fairgrounds, to show the advantages of electric power and how domestic labor could be made easier with its use. The middle photo likely depicts such a demonstration. These demonstrations continued into the 1970s at the cooperative's building on the west bank of the Rum River in Anoka. The building never drew power from the river despite its strategic location.

Left: *Telephone lines often ran along roads and railroads. This lineman was climbing a pole ca. 1910–20 along Highway 10 west of Anoka in what was then known as Itaska.*

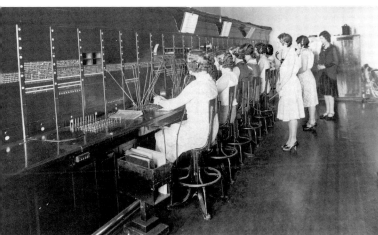

Top: *This photo of Bethel's Main Street is undated, but a general time can be deduced from evidence in the photograph. There are no cars, only horses and wagons, but poles and wires are visible. The poles are for telegraph and telephone wires. The corridor created by train tracks was often followed for putting up the telegraph, and later, the telephone lines. The telephone lines reached the area of Bethel in 1901. Nellie Blain was a farm wife living in nearby Oak Grove in 1905, and she commented frequently about the telephone in her diary. On Wednesday, January 4, 1905, she wrote, ". . . A stormy day does not seem so long now, as it used to before we had the Phone." Other entries in her diary about the telephone lead to speculation that she listened to conversations on the "party line" whether they were intended for her or not.*

Bottom left: *The City of Anoka telephone switchboard was located above the office where patrons paid their bills. In the 1920s, the date of this photo, it was located on First Avenue North. Corinne Vevea is the only person identified; of the three standing, she is in the center.*

Bottom right: *The first telephone switchboard in Constance (Ham Lake) was in the Andrew Simonson home in the early 1900s. Sarah Simonson is shown here at the switchboard.*

Left: *The first family to hook up to the city sewer system in Circle Pines in August 1967. The expansion of city services within Anoka County has brought sewer, water, and gas lines even farther north in the county.*

Bottom left: *The city of Spring Lake Park painted its water tower in a flag motif for the nation's Bicentennial Celebration in 1976. It quickly became a landmark when one of the painters decided to show his love for his estranged wife and painted "Norma" on the tower in five-foot-tall letters, which made headlines all over the metro area. While the new name was temporary and soon removed, the patriotic paint job remained. The city festival of Tower Days began to celebrate distinctive water towers in 1976, and the celebration goes on every year. The paint on Spring Lake Park's water towers remains a local landmark yet today and will into the foreseeable future as the towers received a new coat of red, white, and blue in 2006.*

Bottom right: *Not everyone is in favor of growth or expansion of development. This sign appeared on the corner of County Road 56 and 15th Avenue in Ramsey, urging citizens to vote against the expansion of city water services. If city services are limited, development of large housing areas are restricted with lot sizes and other constraints. This photo was taken in May 1984.*

Top: *Rapid suburbanization began in the 1950s in Anoka County with developers and builders such as Bronson-Erickson, Vern Donnay, and Orrin Thompson, and the era of tract housing had begun. "Tract" housing referred to the plan of a single builder laying out the streets and building homes throughout that particular area. To keep prices affordable, buyers had a limited choice of floor plans, usually only two or three. There were a few options that could be added, but for the most part the houses looked very much alike. Since the developments were done on a large scale, the streets, lot sizes, boulevard trees, and landscaping were also uniform. Part of the concept was to provide all the amenities a suburban community would need: a central water system, parks, a country club with a swimming pool, townhouses, and recreation areas. Small neighborhood stores were encouraged, and schools quickly followed the new homeowners.*

Middle: *These homes on the south side of 109th Avenue in Blaine are built on land that had been sod fields and wetlands before development. As land values rise in Anoka County, farming has declined until only a handful of true working farms are left. This photo was taken in 1992.*

Bottom: *This bird's-eye view of Spring Lake Park in 1975 shows the beginnings of the Fairview housing addition with the high school in the background. Spring Lake Park Independent School District 16 covers all of Spring Lake Park and portions of Blaine and Fridley.*

Right and bottom left and right:
Recycling has long been a part of Anoka County. The early settlers were known to scrap their wagons and use the materials to build shelters. During World War II, drives were held to reuse scrap metal for war and industrial efforts. Today, most cities and townships have extensive programs to encourage their citizens to recycle. Fridley offers curbside pickup of recyclable items, a compost pile for yard waste, and has a television program that demonstrates recycling techniques and the city's services.

Left: *Hartley Medin and Bobby Schieffer of the Crooked Lake 4-H Club were successful in their efforts to gather scrap metal for the war effort of WWII. Because there was a need for metal, scrap drives were organized throughout the nation. The first Anoka County 4-H scrap drive was organized in January 1942, and all twenty-three of the county's 4-H Clubs participated, competing for trophies. The effort netted 101,643 pounds of scrap metal and required nineteen trucks to haul it to the collection point in Minneapolis. The winning club was the Northwest Rousers, which collected 26,363 pounds of scrap metal. There were two more scrap drives that year, and Anoka County exceeded the assigned one thousand-ton quota.*

3

Working:
Anoka County Business and Industry

Commerce is the lifeblood of a community. People need to work to earn money; then they spend money to get things they need. And so life goes. The pictures in this chapter show how entrepreneurs brought business and prosperity to Anoka County.

Every business needs money; thus, banks popped up in communities from Bethel to Columbia Heights to serve both businesses and people in building their dreams.

One consistent industry throughout the county's history centered on food—grocery stores, meat markets, butcher shops, farmers' vegetable stands, bakeries, cafes, restaurants, and even fast food.

Retail was also important—dry goods, shoes, clothing, general stores, hardware and drugstores, and even discount stores such as Zayre Shopper's City peppered communities throughout the county.

People wanted service as well. Barbershops, auto repair, travel, and delivery services popped up to meet the need.

Of course, not all businesses dealt with food, service, and retail. Manufacturing, milling, and construction businesses created jobs for many county residents. Some of the county's proudest employers worked in the defense industry.

And while many don't think of media as business, it certainly is—look at commercials and print ads. The county has been home to radio and newspapers alike.

Today many county residents live here but work elsewhere. It wasn't always that way. The county's strong business history attests to that.

Above: *The Columbia Heights State Bank, pictured here in the 1960s. The bank located at 3982 Central Avenue in Columbia Heights began as the Columbia State Bank in 1923. C. H. Woodward was one of the executive officers when it began and remained for many years. The Columbia Heights State Bank opened in 1937. It eventually became Marquette State Bank, then First Bank, and finally U.S. Bank, as it is in 2007.*

Left: *The State Bank of Bethel opened on Main Street downtown in 1904. It remained in business until 1931.*

Top left: *A growing community would need places for travelers to stay, and this need was filled by the Columbia Hotel. At some point, it was called the Victoria Hotel and included a sign that read "office and club house" on its front corner. Thomas Lowry was involved with a group of men to build this facility at 3980 Fifth Street. The front part of the building was a real estate office when it was built in 1907, but the real business was a private gentleman's clubhouse—a private getaway from the harassment in Minneapolis, which, in the 1920s, was undergoing a cleanup campaign by law enforcement and city officials. Remember, this was the era of prohibition!*

Top right: *The Hughes Hotel, purchased by Henry Hughes in 1907, was originally known as Strong's Hotel. Opened in 1901–02, much of its business came from railroad patrons. However, another steady stream of customers came for the "blind pigs," a veiled reference to an establishment that sold liquor. When it was known as Strong's Hotel, prohibitionists managed to drive the proprietor, Jim Strong, out of town. The building was sold, enlarged, and became the Starkey Hotel in 1902. In later years, people called the hotel "Honeymoon Flats" because of all the newly married couples who began married life in one of its apartments.*

Bottom: *The Night-O-Rest Motel stood on West Main Street and welcomed visitors who passed by on what was then a section of Jefferson Highway and Highway 10. The grounds around the motel were filled with attention-getters such as these little castle-like buildings, a miniature waterfall, and a footbridge. The motel began as a tourist camp; approval from the city to build three small cabins came from the City Council in 1932. The proprietor was F. R. Bergsten, who eventually built on to his tourist camp with an "eat shop" and traditional motel. A well-known landmark was the giant Cali-fornia redwood log he brought in to place beside his hotel. The motel and the property were sold to the Anoka American Legion in 1976 and closed in the early 1980s. The group built their Legion Hall on the site.*

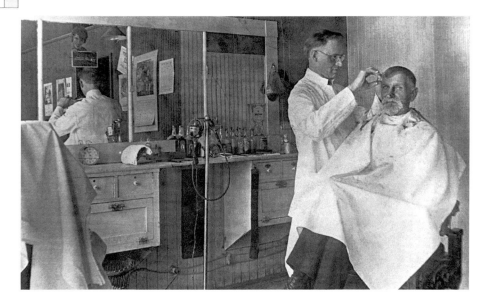

Left: *Andy Meyer ran a barber-shop at 1920 First Avenue South in Anoka in the 1920s.*

Below: *This is the general store run by Iver Soderquist, pictured here behind his counter. The area known as "Soderville" was named for his family. It has never been a separate community but always a distinct part of Ham Lake. This photo is not dated, but Iver died in 1971 at the age of sixty-nine. The Soderquist store heritage in Soderville (Ham Lake) remains in 2007, with the Soderquist Market grocery store located at 17525 Highway 65.*

Top right: *John Ferron came to Anoka from Sweden in 1879. He worked in logging and then for the Washburn Milling Company until 1887, when he opened a clothing store in Anoka. The successful businessman bought out the assets of the Anoka Clothing Company and brought his son, Roy, into the business. The father-and-son team operated the Wear-U-Well shoe and clothing store on Main Street. John died in 1927, and Roy continued the store for a few more years. When the store closed, the building became an ice cream parlor.*

Middle right: *The Central Garage took its name from the road it faced: Central Avenue, today known as Highway 65. The garage still stands at the northwest corner of Highway 65 and Crosstown Boulevard. While the photo is not dated, the towtruck parked in front is a 1925 Hudson.*

Bottom right: *This heating oil and auto repair company was located at 8351 Lake Drive, Lino Lakes.*

Right: *A horse with its wagon and an automobile are both parked outside H. G. Leathers Hardware Store in St. Francis in the early years of the twentieth century. The Leathers family was one of the first families in the Oak Grove and St. Francis areas. H. G. "Henry" was born in Oak Grove in 1858. He graduated from Anoka's high school and attended classes at Carleton College in Northfield, Minnesota. In 1883 he opened his general store on Main Street. By the time of this photo, he was selling John Deere farm equipment, among many other items, as can be seen by his displays in the windows.*

Middle: *The Nowthen Store has been a fixture in Burns Township from the days when groceries and mail were picked up by horse and buggy until today. This photo, with both old and new vehicles parked out front, says they are busy.*

Bottom left: *John Augustson came from Sweden and started this butcher shop in Grow Township. He lived in quarters at the back of the store before he was married in 1910.*

Bottom right: *The Union Grocery store, ca. 1900, supplied the needs of people living in the area of Oak Grove known as Cedar. In front of the store are John Ostlund and Mr. Tucker.*

Top left: *Grandpa's Roadside Stand pictured in 1992. William Waldoch bought a farm in Lino Lakes in 1917 to raise chickens and grow vegetables, which he sold at a roadside stand. With hard work by four generations of the family, the vegetable stand was successful and grew to become a garden and retail center with five greenhouses and a retail store. Nearly all the plants sold are grown on the farm Grandpa William started in 1917. The family still keeps Grandpa's Roadside Stand as a part of their tradition.*

Top right: *Ted's Store, at 13130 Crooked Lake Boulevard in Coon Rapids, began many years past with Ted Buzzelli, who offered basic grocery items in the neighborhood, intending to save people a trip to the bigger stores. After his death in 1983, his wife, Millie, took over. She continues to run the store in the same way Ted always did, saying the kids are her favorite part. The store is still in operation in 2007. This photo was taken in 1992.*

Bottom left: *Zayre, pictured in 1968, was an early discount variety store, selling everything from tools to toys and clothing to car parts. It was located in the "hole" on the west side of Central Avenue (4300 block) in Columbia Heights. Another Zayre's Shopper's City was in Coon Rapids. The stores closed in the late 1970s.*

Bottom right: *Carrie Belle Augustson, Corrina Augustson, and Hazel Augustson are pictured outside the Johnsville Grocery store ca. 1929. The Johnsville neighborhood was in the area of Highway 65 and 242 in Blaine. Though it was never incorporated as a separate community, Johnsville had shops, businesses, and homes.*

Right: *Goss's Café, ca. 1925, stood at the southeast corner of Jackson Street and First Avenue in Anoka. William Goss is pictured on the left. The original image of this photograph was taken as a glass slide and was shown at the movie theater through a large projector to advertise local businesses.*

Middle left: *This small store at Mississippi Street and East River Road in Fridley ca. 1920 was started by August E. Grosslien, a soda pop wholesaler and a near beer distributor for the Golden Grain Juice Company, which later became Grain Belt Brewing.*

Bottom left: *Robert and Delores Grosslien, the children of August and Caroline Grosslien, are standing at left on the porch of the store. The family lived above the store.*

Bottom right: *Advertising card for Brezler's Bakery in Anoka. The "domestic" label may have referred to locally grown wheat.*

Top left: *Soderville offered more than hot dogs and root beer. Jacobson's Confectionery sold gas, lunches, soft drinks, ice cream, and beer.*

Top right: *Imagine buying a dozen hot dogs or hamburgers for fifty cents! That was the going rate when this photo was taken in the 1930s or 1940s of Margaret Soderquist-Livgard, whose parents were Bill and Minnie Soderquist. Their family helped give the area of Ham Lake along Highway 65 its nickname of "Soderville."*

Middle left: *The Laddie Lake Inn was an eating establishment on the east shore of Laddie Lake on the west side of Central Avenue in Spring Lake Park.*

Middle right: *This sign, proclaiming Lino Lakes the "Gateway to the Twin Cities" in 1961, leans against a Lino Cabinet Company truck parked in front of a popular eating establishment, Chicken in the Basket, where one could buy food, groceries, and more.*

Bottom: *Elmer's Place in Cedar was a popular place to stop for a treat in the East Bethel and Oak Grove area. This photo is from a 1950s postcard.*

Top: *This strip mall, pictured in 1992 on the north side of 109th Avenue in the 1000 block of Blaine, used to be sod fields. The anchor for the mall is the BeBop Café, a bar and eatery with volleyball courts, softball fields, and other competitive sport venues. Teams and leagues keep the fields and courts busy in the summer months.*

Middle: *Employees of Central Park Warehouse Liquors, on the corner at 8101 Highway 65, are pictured in 2003. In 1956, Spring Lake Park, wanting to control the sale of liquor within its borders, established the first municipal liquor store. The profits were used to keep property taxes low and to build sidewalks. There have been three municipal liquor stores over the years. The current one is off-sale only.*

Left: *One of the first fast food restaurant chains in Anoka County was a McDonald's on Central Avenue in Columbia Heights. It was flipping burgers by the thousands already in the early 1960s.*

Left: *Bill and Alice Eberman are pictured on the front steps of Happy Corner in Burns in 1990. Francis and Alice Koehler built the 3.2 beer establishment in 1938. It was open seven days a week, and even if you had cow manure on your boots, you were still welcome and comfortable there. Bill Eberman was the Koehlers' handyman. Happy Corner closed when Alice Eberman died in 1991.*

Below: *Leonard Sandstrom is standing by a Benson and Peterson General Store delivery truck used to take merchandise to customers in the Ham Lake area.*

Top: *Uriah Sparks Pratt is pictured ca. 1907–18. Pratt, the son of Elias W. Pratt, worked with his father as a teamster in the Goss Logging Camp on Cass Lake. Later, he took over his brother's Dave's Standard Oil Service in 1907. In 1918 he left the company after being elected county sheriff. At the time, most oil was purchased by railroad companies. In the 1910s, automobiles were gaining in popularity but were still considered luxury items.*

Middle: *Everett Ward stands in front of a Veerac delivery vehicle ca. 1912–14. The name is an acronym for Valveless Explosion, Every Revolution Air Cooled. The company built these motorized vehicles in a factory on North Ferry Street in Anoka. They were used mostly for delivery and hauling jobs, but the company also made a farm version called a tractor.*

Below: *These men are posed in front of the Veerac building in Anoka. The vehicles they are posed on appear to run on tracks, but the Veerac was not restricted to them. The company made several kinds of vehicles in addition to small motors, power pumps, washing machines, and small farm implements, such as a fanning mill.*

Top left: *The transmitter building for WCCO, village of Coon Rapids, ca. 1950s.*

Top right: *WCCO's radio tower in Anoka Township, 1925. WCCO Radio built its first transmitter in Coon Rapids (then Anoka Township) in 1924. The first transmission of the 300-foot tower, with 5,000 watts of power, was President Calvin Coolidge's 1925 inaugural address. In 1932 the tower was replaced with a 654-foot, 50,000-watt transmitter.*

Middle left: *The Ward Transfer Company. The Ward family goes back more than four generations in Anoka County, with William and Rebecca Ward settling in what is now Ramsey. The company was founded in 1902 by four of their sons and was the first licensed common carrier in Minnesota. The first shipment, carried by John E. Ward, was a load of shoes bound from Anoka to Minneapolis and pulled by horse. By 1912 the company had purchased a made-in-Anoka Veerac truck but would maintain a team of horses until 1925. John was the last of the original brothers to sell his share of the company, in 1960. The name continued until the 1970s, when a Wisconsin firm purchased the company.*

Bottom left: *Ward Transfer workshop ca. 1925–26.*

Top: *Bridge, dam, and flour mill in St. Francis. Almost as soon as there were entrepreneurs in the county, they had sought out the water power available from the Rum River. Albert Woodbury and, later, his brother, John, were involved in the milling of flour in St. Francis.*

Bottom left: Anoka County Union *pressroom in the Union Building ca. 1965. The* Union *began when George Gray purchased the* Anoka Star *in 1865. He later sold the paper to his partner, Granville Pease, in 1866. The first location was a wooden building at Main and Ferry in Anoka. They lost their second building at First and Main in an 1884 fire. By 1907, they had built their longtime home on the east bank of the Rum River. In 1953, they moved to the Union Building on Jackson Street, where they stayed until moving to a larger facility on Coon Rapids Boulevard. The Pease family owned the paper for four generations until Thomas Pease sold it to Elmer Andersen's ECM Publishers, which still owns the paper today.*

Bottom right: *A group of courageous types pose on a pile of sawed lumber in the yard of Anoka's Washburn Sawmill ca. 1890.*

Above: *Federal Cartridge in Anoka ca. 1925. It began operation in 1917 under the direction of brothers Harry and Lewis Sherman. Over the next few years, after the business had disappointing sales, the Shermans severed their ties, and it shut down in 1920. In 1922 Charles L. Horn took over, and the organization made a remarkable turnaround. Business continued to improve, and World War II made the company into a national powerhouse and one of the county's largest employers. In its long history, Federal has been recognized for its achievements in ammunition production and development, marketing, and advertising, and was commended by the U.S. Department of Defense for achievement in quality production in 1944. The original building still remains on the campus.*

Middle: *A tube-rolling machine at Federal Cartridge ca. 1950.*

Bottom: *The North Star Shoe Company, established in the mid-1880s, is pictured in 1899. The company did poorly in its early years and shut down for an extended period until 1897, when Granville Pease facilitated the city's purchase of the factory. After five years of successful operation, the city returned the deed to the factory. But the business survived only until 1910. After the buyout, the company, with 100 employees, turned out 700 pairs of shoes every weekday. In a ten-hour workday, it produced a shoe every twenty-five seconds. By the time it was finished, a shoe passed through as many as twenty pairs of hands. Early on, the plant hired women; however, pay rates between men and women were not quite equal. Most of the women were employed in the stitching department. The average pay for a woman was $3 to $9 per week, while a man typically made up to $12.50 per week.*

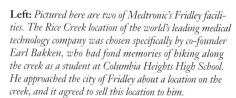

Left: *Pictured here are two of Medtronic's Fridley facilities. The Rice Creek location of the world's leading medical technology company was chosen specifically by co-founder Earl Bakken, who had fond memories of hiking along the creek as a student at Columbia Heights High School. He approached the city of Fridley about a location on the creek, and it agreed to sell this location to him.*

Bottom left: *Medtronic, the world's leading medical technology company, is headquartered in Fridley. Co-founders Earl Bakken and Palmer Hermundslie started the business in 1949 in Bakken's Fridley garage while he worked part time in a hospital and did graduate work in electrical engineering. In 1957, the company perfected the first wearable external pacemaker to regulate a human heart. The pacemaker used the circuitry design for a transistorized metronome. Three years later, they developed the first reliable, long-term implantable pacemaker. Since then, Medtronic has remained on the leading edge of medical technology. Other notable firsts for the company include the first implantable drug delivery system designed to provide medication directly to the spinal cord to treat spasticity and malignant and nonmalignant pain, and an Internet-based system that allows cardiac device patients to transmit data from their implanted devices.*

Right: *Reed and Sherwood lumber company, which opened in 1875 with a steam mill, had an initial output of 90,000 board feet in ten hours. The company, which specialized in sash and door trimmings—ordered through a catalog—was located in Anoka just north of the railroad track on the west side of Ferry Street. By 1879 it had a payroll of $5,000 per month—a large amount of money at the time.*

Below: *The Aveda Corporation, founded by Horst Rechelbacher in 1978, is a worldwide leader in the cosmetics industry. Headquartered in Blaine, the company has a commitment to environmentally ethical policies.*

4

Learning:
Anoka County Education

If commerce is the lifeblood of a community, education is the heart that pumps the blood, and it has always played an important role in Anoka County's history, as the pictures in this chapter show.

Rural communities faced challenges in educating farm children, who were needed to help at home. One-room schools housed all the students from grades one through eight, and one teacher was expected to teach each grade every day. Add that there were no central heat or air, paper notebooks, or hot lunch program—well, you get the idea of how dedicated students and teachers had to be to stay in school.

We often think of public schools in relation to the history of education, but parochial schools, typically affiliated with a church, contributed much to the education of the county's young people, too.

It's obvious county residents appreciated the importance of education. Just look at all the communities that had schools: Bethel, East Bethel, Linwood, Columbus, Ham Lake, Anoka, Johnsville, and Ramsey are all represented in this chapter.

The old saying goes, "If you can read this, thank a teacher." But school is more than just learning lessons. It's also sports, extracurricular activities, and graduation.

And after high school graduation, there's more school to attend if a student wants to go on.

Back when most students quit school after their elementary grades, Anoka had a college—the Anoka Business College.

That college may be gone, but the county currently boasts two more colleges—Anoka Ramsey Community College and Anoka Technical College.

We're where we are because of those who have come before us. They laid the foundation in education, and we get to keep the learning going through projects such as this book.

Top: *Anoka County has long contained parochial schools, most associated with various churches. This group is the St. Anne's Fife and Drum Corps, pictured on the east side of the St. Anne's School and Convent in Anoka. First row, far left, is Ruth Witte; back row, right to left, are Bernadine Ziegler, Elaine Witte, Phyllis Lahn, and Mary Witte.*

Left: *Sister Albertine, one of the nuns who taught at St. Anne's School. St. Anne's School was affiliated with St. Stephen's Catholic Church in Anoka.*

Left: *Bethel School was built in 1904–05.*

Bottom left: *School District 40 was located in Section 8 in Bethel Township in the early 1900s. The school held classes from first to eighth grade. The teacher, unidentified, can be seen in the back row at the right edge of the door.*

Bottom right: *Former teachers in East Bethel. Before Bethel and East Bethel were incorporated as separate communities, many referred to the area as simply "Bethel," which can lead to much confusion. The collage of photos shown here was identified simply as "Former school teachers, East Bethel." Situations such as these make a good case for identifying photographs fully, including names, dates, and places on the margins or back of the photograph with an archivally safe pencil.*

Top: *The end of the school year each spring was a time to celebrate with a picnic. This photo was taken at the school in Ham Lake ca. 1892.*

Middle left: *Andrew Grubb's class at the Mare School in 1938. Grubbs is in the center back row.*

Middle right: *Mother's Day was a special day to celebrate in the Linwood School District 35. Based on the number of adults in the photo, it is believed the children brought their mothers to the school for an event that day.*

Bottom: *Johnsville was an area in northern Blaine west and north of the intersection of Highways 242 and 65. Shirley Atkins-Johnson taught the class in the 1920s.*

Top: *The high school in Anoka offered some specialty classes for students. These are agricultural students ca. 1913.*

Middle: *Columbus school in 1920, taught by Marie Waldoch. The students must have all dressed in their best; see the ties on a couple of the boys. And note the haircuts on the girls—the 1920 "bobbed" haircut is everywhere.*

Bottom: *School District 6 was in Columbus Township. Though this photo is undated, this class of students was probably attending school ca. 1900.*

Top left: *The one-room schoolhouse that served as the school for District 28 in Ramsey was built of brick and served students for many years. After it was no longer used for classes, the Town Board of Ramsey continued to hold city meetings there until 1976. The building is listed on the National Register of Historic Places.*

Top right: *The one-room schoolhouse that was Lino Elementary School stood on the corner of Main Street and Lake Drive.*

Left: *Anoka-Ramsey is not the first institution of higher learning in the county. In 1885, the Anoka Business College was operating downtown. Another advanced-education facility, the Normal School, helped eighth-grade graduates learn to be teachers. Normal training was not required to be a teacher, but usually teachers who had the extra training received higher pay.*

Top: *This photo of the 1941 Columbia Heights High School football team was featured in the yearbook. The team only scored twice during the entire season of nine games, but it was enough for them to win their homecoming game against North St. Paul. The yearbook article noted that the team was mostly made up of tenth- and eleventh-graders, so there were "promising players" for the coming years. Because of conservation efforts and shortages due to World War II, the staff was forced to produce the yearbook on a ditto machine and glue a few significant photographs on the pages.*

Middle: *Homecoming 1941 at Columbia Heights High School was especially sweet with a win on the football field. The festivities included a parade, music and marching programs, a dance, and the crowning of Queen Olga Leschisin. She was attended by Lila Bunders, Alice Dzaman, LeRayne Fetcek, and Helyn Teno.*

Bottom: *Columbia Heights High School in 1941.*

Above: *These students from Washington School in Anoka were boarding a bus to go ice skating ca. early 1980s.*

Left: *Tip-off at a 1974 Anoka–Ramsey Community College basketball game during the 1974–75 season. The school began as a "junior" college in the Centennial school district area in 1965, and the first classes were held in a wing of Centennial High School. The formal campus was constructed on the bank of the Mississippi River in Coon Rapids and soon grew to be a well-attended local "community" college offering two-year degrees and all the amenities of college life, including sports. A classic example of the community college system that grew and flourished in the 1960s, the school now has campuses in Coon Rapids and Cambridge.*

Top: *A wrestler from St. Francis High School gets advice from coach Gene Yanke ca. 1960s-1970s.*

Middle: *A game of Anoka High School football played under the lights of Goodrich Field ca. 1939. The field is between Fourth and Fifth Avenues and Madison and Military Road in Anoka.*

Bottom: *Swimming was a popular competitive sport for girls in the 1970s. The swimmer in the striped suit is Patty Hagman of Blaine High School, 1975.*

Top: *Centennial High School's graduating class of 1961. Centennial is a part of Independent School District 12 and serves students in all or portions of Centerville, Circle Pines, Lexington, and Lino Lakes.*

Bottom left: *Centennial school students participated in the first Earth Day by cleaning up the school grounds on April 30, 1970. The environment-friendly spirit may have been influenced by the city of Circle Pines, which began in 1945 as a cooperative community to provide affordable housing through mass production of homes. Profits would be shared by the members, all of whom would be part of the community. The plan included adult education opportunities, nurseries, educational, and recreational activities, and each house would front a park or a walkway. The commercial facilities and services were to be cooperatively owned by the members, as would all municipal utilities. Profits, if there were any, were to be divided among the members. But the dream did not work out as the original planners wanted, and the community incorporated as a traditional village in 1950.*

Bottom right: *Ed Bloomstrand is shown here with school children at a food drive held in the early 1980s.*

On December 6, 1966, people in the Anoka–Hennepin School District 11 voted to accept the proposed idea of a vocational educational facility. The site had already been selected—the old Char-Gale building on Highway 10 on Anoka's west side. The company had left the site a year earlier and sold it to the school district. It grew to be one of the largest technical colleges in the area and the only one located in Anoka County. It is known as the Anoka Technical College in 2007.

Howard Rosenwinkel, the director of vocational education in the 1960s, received much of the credit for envisioning the Technical Education Center, a place where students could obtain hands-on occupational opportunities.

5

Working the Land:
Anoka County Agriculture

Throughout most of Anoka County's history, agriculture has been a critical part. The pictures in this chapter show you many of the ways agriculture supported county residents.

Think agriculture, and crops probably come to mind. Corn is obvious, and winter wheat isn't too surprising, but did you realize the county grew wire grass? What's wire grass? It was used to make rugs.

Many county residents remember the truck farms and how young people worked on them before they were old enough to hold other jobs. Potatoes were a huge truck-farm crop. But did you know Anoka County has a strong history of making excellent starch from its potatoes?

When farmers grew crops, they eventually had the harvest. Farm equipment was so expensive that often farmers couldn't afford to own all the implements and equipment they needed, so they shared to get the harvest in.

If you didn't think crops when you thought agriculture, you may have thought livestock. And certainly the obvious livestock of horses and cattle played a big part in the county's agriculture. But there were also lambs, chickens, turkeys, eggs, dairy (creameries and co-ops), and 4-H programs.

Times change, as all the pictures in this book show us. Today, land used for agriculture is being used to build housing as the county population grows.

It's a fair assumption we will never return to the days of agriculture the county once knew. But we can gaze on the pictures in this chapter and remember farming was once a typical way of life in Anoka County.

Left: *This woman in East Bethel is helping shock grain by hand ca. 1920–30. Many of Anoka County's early farmers depended on their families for labor, and women worked in the fields as well as the house.*

Middle left: *Children did their share of work on farms, adding to the meaning of "family farm." These two youths in the East Bethel area are working with a type of horse-drawn digger ca. 1920s-1930s.*

Middle right: *W. E. Bean in his cornfield, 1941.*

Bottom: *The Rufus Downs farm in Ramsey ca. 1910.*

Top left: *Camp 3 flopping crew, known as "rubber backs," for the American Twine Company, Columbus, ca. 1890. Wire grass, grown in the swamps and bogs of Anoka County, was tall (up to three feet) and wiry (it was easy to cut your hands on it). Harvesting the grass sometimes required horses to wear special bog shoes to avoid sinking and getting stuck. The American Twine Company, opened in the early 1890s, owned ten thousand acres of land in Columbus Township. Initially, the wire grass grown in the area was intended for twine; however, it was not a good match. Instead, the grass was used in making rugs. After World War I, rugs were imported for a cheaper price. This, combined with lower water levels in the bogs as a result of ditching, brought an end to most of the wire grass production.*

Top right: *Loading wire grass onto a train car in Forest Lake ca. 1890.*

Middle: *John Lindbloom (in overalls) and Albin Greenberg, undated. Greenberg worked on his father's farm in Burns and did mechanical repairs for friends and neighbors on the side. After marrying Edith Skogquist in 1924, he moved to Minneapolis for a short time to work as a mechanic. He returned to Burns to open a garage and gas station in Nowthen. His sons, Donald and Harvey, eventually took over the business and expanded into selling farm implements. The business survives to this day as Greenberg Implement Inc. The Greenberg family has been a fixture in Nowthen since the 1920s.*

Right: *Henry Stack in a winter wheat field in Ramsey, 1942.*

Right: *Old William Staples' farm in Grow Township, undated. One of the Staples boys is seated atop the swatter, a farm implement that pushes grain against a cutting blade to be harvested. The Staples family arrived in Anoka County in the late 1850s and claimed land. Sarah Foster Staples, wife of Ralph, is seated in the buggy.*

Middle: *Oscar Swanson's farm in St. Francis, undated. Harvest time was a community event that brought neighbors together to share camaraderie, labor, and equipment. Sharing resources was an economic necessity for most farmers.*

Bottom left: *Billy Milliman, standing on the tractor, and Oscar Swanson, standing at the far right, at Swanson's farm in St. Francis. The men are posing in front of a steam tractor ca. 1930.*

Bottom right: *This early farm scene shows threshing near St. Francis. The third man on the left is Oscar Swanson.*

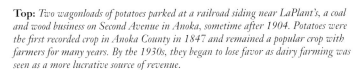
St. Francis Potato Starch Factory, St. Francis, Minn.

Top: *Two wagonloads of potatoes parked at a railroad siding near LaPlant's, a coal and wood business on Second Avenue in Anoka, sometime after 1904. Potatoes were the first recorded crop in Anoka County in 1847 and remained a popular crop with farmers for many years. By the 1930s, they began to lose favor as dairy farming was seen as a more lucrative source of revenue.*

Middle left: *The St. Francis Potato Starch Factory ca. early 1900s. Three potato factories opened in Anoka County in the last twenty years of the nineteenth century—two in Anoka and one in St. Francis—processing farmers' excess and lower-grade potatoes into starch. In October 1900, the* Anoka Herald *reported: "These days the starch factories are the busiest places in the county, for in them about 9,000 bushels of potatoes are made into starch every twenty-four hours. . . . In all probability the factories will furnish a market for nearly a million bushels of tubers this year, which is not bad for a county of this size."*

Middle right: *The Walburn family was deeply involved with the 4-H program in Anoka County. Their children, shown here, are: Irma, Cora Belle, Willard, and Donald. Irma won the county fair's purebred live lamb class with her Shropshire sheep named Dolly. Donald won second at the fair in the Guernsey calf competition.*

Right: *Ed Lindstrom with hogs on his Soderville farm, 1941. Soderville is a neighborhood in Ham Lake.*

Left: *Red Oaks Ruby, one of L. J. Greenwald's prized milk cows.*

Middle: *Free-range chickens on one of George Ghostley's several farms in Anoka County ca. 1940s. In 1936 alone, Ghostley Pearl Chickens hatched more than 300,000 chicks and sold more than 260,000 of them in boxes of 100 chicks each, shipped by parcel post.*

Bottom left: *Breeding houses on Ghostley farm, probably in Coon Rapids, ca. 1940s. George Ghostley graduated from the University of Minnesota with a degree in medicine, but his health prevented him from practicing. In 1918 he raised and selectively bred hens through trapnesting. His Ghostley Pearl Chickens (named for his wife, Pearl, not their white appearance) became known worldwide for their superior laying qualities.*

Bottom right: *L. J. Greenwald and herd of milking greenhorns at his Lake George farm ca. 1900–05. L. J., son of Aaron Greenwald, believed to the first volunteer for the Union Army in the Civil War, was a well-known and prosperous farmer and businessman in the county. A longtime employee of the First National Bank of Anoka, he also farmed in Oak Grove, where he received many awards for his cattle and horses.*

Right: *Cow no. 89 on the Ray Jones dairy farm in St. Francis, 2004.*

Middle left: *Anoka County had many small creameries at the turn of the twentieth century. Because most milk was transported by horse-drawn wagon, a creamery needed to be located nearby so the milk could be processed quickly and not spoil. The smaller creameries began disappearing in the 1910s as they faced competition from larger centralized ones that could take dairy in by rail, and as smaller farms were able to use mechanized home cream separation.*

Middle right: *Shadick residence and St. Francis Creamery. In the last years of the nineteenth century, creameries usually operated as cooperatives, but dairy farmers saw technology changing the process. For example, a mechanical separator separated milk from cream faster than the traditional gravity process that had been used.*

Bottom: *Mulcare Homestead, at 51st and Central in Columbia Heights, 1914. Today's Columbia Heights, bordering Minneapolis' northeast boundary, looks much different from its agrarian roots.*

These farms in Burns, Blaine, Ramsey, and Linwood are among the few remaining family farms in the county. Land uses were changing dramatically in the last half of the twentieth century in Anoka County. As the county and the Twin Cities metro area experienced a population boom, land that had produced crops for generations was now needed for housing. The photos were taken as part of a 2004–05 agricultural survey that the Anoka County Historical Society conducted with a grant from the county Agricultural Extension Service.

Bottom right: *Development of farm land at 213th and Xeon in Burns Township, 2004, demonstrates how Anoka County is growing. A housing development can be seen sprouting up just beyond the barn.*

6

Service and Sacrifice:
Anoka County Military Service

*I*n the past 150 years, Anoka County residents' service to the country has been very impressive. You'll want to read each caption and look closely at each picture because this chapter is about service and sacrifice to ensure the United States survives.

The Civil War came shortly after Minnesota reached statehood. And a young man from Anoka was the first to step forward and volunteer to fight. Unfortunately, as happened to so many who volunteered over the 150 years, he never came home.

One did come home—with a Congressional Medal of Honor. He was awarded the medal for throwing himself on top of a grenade just before it exploded to save his fellow marines during World War II. (He survived.)

Some veterans continue to serve their communities even after they retire from the military, as one Hilltop mayor did.

There's an armory in Anoka today. Other armories stood in town before this one because Anoka County has sent service men and women to all these wars and conflicts: Civil and Indian Wars, Spanish-American War, Mexican Border Conflict, World War I, World War II, the Korean Conflict, Vietnam, Desert Storm, and Operation Iraqi Freedom.

Even the Cold War brought county residents into serving in the Civil Defense.

With so many veterans, it's only fitting there are organizations to support and work on their behalf. After the Civil War, the county had the Grand Army of the Republic (GAR). Today we have the Veterans of Foreign Wars (VFW) and the American Legion.

Anoka County can stand proud among Americans. Throughout its 150-year history, residents served, and served well.

Top left: *Aaron Greenwald, the first man to enlist in the Union Army. Green-wald was a twenty-eight-year-old miller living in Anoka when the opening shots of the Civil War were fired. Governor Alexander Ramsey offered 1,000 men from Minnesota to put down the rebellion—the 1st Minnesota Volunteer Infantry still yet to be formed. Ramsey telegraphed a message to St. Paul, where it was given to a messenger on horseback to deliver to Willis Gorman, a lawyer involved in a court case in the 4th District Court, then being held in Anoka. When the message arrived in Anoka, volunteers were asked for, and Greenwald heeded the call. Greenwald was killed at the Battle of Gettysburg in 1863. He has many descendants in Anoka County yet today.*

Top right: *Lucius Pratt served as a bugler in the 2nd Minnesota Battery of Light Artillery during the Civil War. He was from Anoka County, as were more men in the 2nd Battery than from any other county in the state. When the artillery battery was forming up in winter 1861–62, Albert Woodbury of Anoka was helping to recruit men from his home county. Woodbury was one of the very early settlers in St. Francis before he moved to Anoka. He was involved in the milling and water rights in both communities before he went off to serve as a lieutenant in the 2nd Battery. Pratt survived the war and returned home to Anoka County, where he spent the rest of his life. Woodbury was not so fortunate; he died from wounds suffered in the Battle at Chickamauga, Georgia, in October 1863. Anoka County was quite proud of the fact that there never had to be a "draft" of men to fill their assigned quota of men to serve in the Civil War. There were always enough volunteers to meet the required need; they were enticed by patriotic duty, cash bounties, and the Homestead Acts that promised them land for enlisting. More than three hundred men who listed Anoka County as their home when they enlisted fought in the Civil War before it was over, some reenlisting to serve more than once.*

Left: *Fritz A. Peterson was a first sergeant in Company B, 3rd Minnesota Infantry in 1917 when this photo was taken. He had been a member of the National Guard for two years and had seen active duty along the Mexican border during the border conflict and was recalled to active duty for WWI. Peterson remained in the guard and was recalled to active duty many times during his forty-one-year military service, eventually rising to the rank of brigadier general. When not on active duty, Peterson worked as an accountant and lived on Branch Street in Anoka.*

Left: *Richard Sorenson of Anoka is shown greeting his mother after getting off the train in Minneapolis on August 4, 1944. Three Anoka County men, all marines, were awarded the Congressional Medal of Honor. All three were on islands in the Pacific theater fighting against the Japanese when an enemy hand grenade was thrown in the midst of a group of marines. James LaBelle, Richard Kraus, and Sorenson, all from Anoka County, each covered the grenade with their bodies to protect their fellow marines. In each case, the grenade exploded. Sorenson was the only one of the three to survive his action.*

Below: *James Carroll passing through Peruwlez, Belgium, on May 14, 1944, and returning to the city in 1995. On May 14, 1944, Carroll, a reconnaissance scout for the Army's 628th Tank Destroyer Battalion, rode through the town of Peruwlez in advance of his tank unit. Alone, Carroll was greeted by the town citizens and showered with flowers, chocolates, and cognac as a liberating hero. His name and this image developed mythic status. Rumors of his death made their way back to Peruwlez, and his legend grew further. But Carroll survived the war and served in the Army until 1965 before retiring as a sergeant first class. After his retirement, he settled in Hilltop and served as the city's mayor 1974–77. In 1994, Peruwlez wanted to find Carroll's grave but instead found him alive and well in Alabama. Carroll said he had no specific recollection of the town, but the town invited him back on several occasions to honor him before his death.*

Left: *Civil Defense sirens at the Circle Pines Fire Station in the early 1960s. The sirens were first installed to warn of attacks during the Cold War, but using them for storm warnings soon outweighed their nuclear-warning value.*

Middle: *Anoka National Guard members wait for their troop train at the Great Northern Depot on January 22, 1951. The members had marched from the Armory on Main Street to the train depot near 7th Avenue, where they were taken to Camp Rucker, Alabama, for training before going to Korea.*

Bottom: *Anoka County's National Guard Armory was built in 1914 and served as the headquarters for Company B, Battery B and F during the Spanish–American War, the Mexican Border Conflict, and WWI before the structure was destroyed in a 1939 tornado. The guard members used the Knights of Columbus Hall until they were recalled for service in WWII, but the armory was not rebuilt until late 1946, when news arrived that Anoka was to be the home of the 125th Field Artillery Battalion. They met in the commission chambers of Anoka's City Hall until the present armory building was completed.*

Right: *Soldier Dennis Berg of Burns served in Vietnam as a military truck driver in 1966. While records were not kept in individual county lists by the Department of Defense, it is known that at least thirty-three men from Anoka County lost their lives during the fighting in Vietnam. Hundreds of others served in the military. The 1960s brought turmoil to the entire United States, including Anoka County. The Vietnam War saw many people taking sides as to the reasons for fighting in Southeast Asia. Some citizens protested, some enlisted, some were drafted, some ignored the conflict, some considered going to Canada, some were too old, and others were too young, but the rapid pace of change and the Vietnam War touched many lives in the county.*

Below: *In April 1991, Nowthen held its first-ever parade, which was hailed as a welcome-home parade for the troops of Desert Storm.*

Left and middle: *The National Guard unit in Anoka County was activated in 2004 to participate in Operation Iraqi Freedom, where it served for just over a year. Many dignitaries and officials from across the county joined families to welcome home the troops in March 2005.*

Bottom: *This photo shows the home of Post 334 of the American Legion that serves veterans from Coon Rapids. The first veterans organizations in Anoka County were the Grand Army of the Republic (GAR) posts, established after the Civil War. These were organizations composed solely of Union Army veterans. They became a political force in securing pensions for soldiers, widows, and orphans. As these men aged, the posts began to close, but more wars had already created veterans not eligible for the GAR.*

The Veterans of Foreign Wars of the United States traces its roots back to 1899. That year, veterans of the Spanish–American War (1898) and the Philippine Insurrection (1899–1902) founded local organizations to secure rights and benefits for their service. Congress chartered the VFW in 1936.

The American Legion followed the path set by the GAR in working to secure benefits and for veterans other than those of the Civil War. It received its charter from Congress in 1919.

Left: *This GAR Hall stood in Linwood and served the community until the last Civil War veteran in the county passed away.*

Below: *The Grand Army of the Republic (GAR) was a veterans organization made up of Northern veterans of the American Civil War. Anoka County was home to several GAR posts, where veterans would meet, hold events, and plan projects much as the American Legion does today. The city of Anoka had the only GAR home specifically for women. Wives, sisters, and mothers of Union veterans were cared for at this home on West Main Street.*

7

Time for Rest and Play:
Anoka County Recreation

Anoka County residents worked hard, studied hard, and served well, but they also knew how to play. The pictures in this chapter will bring smiles and fond memories to some and questions and wonder to others, but every picture attests to the county's rich history of recreation.

Minnesota is known for its lakes, and Anoka County boasts a few lakes itself. Lake George in Oak Grove has been one of *the* places to go for recreation. Golden Lake in Circle Pines is fun, too. The county's rivers offer relaxation in the form of fishing.

Another water recreation destination is Bunker Beach Water Park, part of the Bunker Hills Regional Park run by Anoka County Parks and Recreation.

Another form of entertainment comes from theater—both live and movie house. During the 1920s, the Windego Park Open Air Theatre in Anoka was very impressive, as was Forest Park in Columbia Heights with its boxing and vaudeville in the 1890s.

In the 1940s, the indoor movie theater in Anoka was the Green Theater. Outdoor (drive-in) theaters were popular in Blaine, Fridley, Coon Rapids, and Columbia Heights. Unfortunately, they became history when the value of the land became more than the value of the business.

Santa Claus Town, west of Anoka, drew children of all ages during the 1950s. Greenhaven Golf Course in Anoka began drawing golfers in 1937 and continues to do so today.

The Carlos Avery Game Farm in Columbus offers a history mixed with excellence as a game farm and horror as a crime scene.

Some of the most fun can be had at community celebrations, fairs, and festivals. The county holds a large fair a mile north of downtown Anoka. And Anoka is known nationally as the Halloween Capital of the World—it's even been on national television several times because of that claim.

Community celebrations such as Circle Pines' Hobo Days, Linwood's Family Fun Fest, Columbia Heights' (with Hilltop participating) Jamboree, St. Francis' Pioneer Days, Spring Lake Park's Tower Days, and so many more around the county offer some of the best old-fashioned fun around.

It's fitting that a county filled with such a rich history also remembers to have some fun along the way.

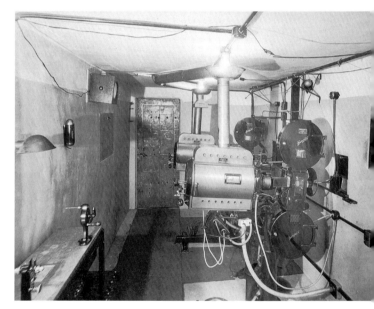

Top left: *The Pancake Inn on Lake George, Oak Grove, ca. 1906. Set upon the lake's west shore, it was built in 1904. Opened by R. G. Chase, editor of the* Anoka Herald, *the Inn consisted of one ten-by-twelve-foot room with electric lights and a "long distance telephone." Chase wrote that it was the "scene of weekly jollifications."*

Top right: *This pavilion, located on Sandy Beach in Oak Grove, was quite the place in its day. It was one of the largest pavilions in the area and was built for people staying in the cottages or by groups from around the area. Gasoline lamps lit the pavilion by night, and there was a stage, room for dancing, and seats all around. On one end there was a "confectionery stand where one may buy ice cream, cigars, candies, soft drinks, and souvenirs of the place."*

Bottom left: *Windego Park Open Air Theatre, Anoka, ca. 1920. Built in 1914, this Greek-style theater on the banks of the Rum River came out of the "City Beautiful" movement that was popular following Chicago's 1893 Columbian Exposition. Designed by the famed architectural firm Purcell and Elmslie, the theater originally had a canvas awning system that was later destroyed. For much of its early existence, the theater, because of its picturesque setting, was used for live theater, musical performances, graduation ceremonies, and movies.*

Bottom right: *Projection room of the Green Theatre, Anoka, ca. 1940. Opened by C. D. Green & Son on December 3, 1914, the theater, located on Main Street, was built to present live theater performances, but, like many such facilities, it started showing motion pictures in the 1920s. The exterior of the building exhibited beveled leaded glass, copper, and iridescent glass. When it opened, the lobby featured a mosaic tile floor, a portable mahogany box office, and the theater provided Circassian walnut opera chairs. It closed its doors in 1951 and was turned into a retail store.*

Forest Park was built by Mr. and Mrs. S. H. Kahm in the mid-1890s and was strategically located near the end of the streetcar line, between 7th and Washington Streets and 40th and 41st Avenues. It was quite the entertainment center, hosting boxing matches, dances, a vaudeville stage, a boardwalk, and a fountain with colored lights at night. It was also home to the first movie theater in Columbia Heights. Church services and weddings were held there, though some people began to think it brought the wrong sort of people to Columbia Heights. By the 1920s, an "anti-Forest Park" movement was gaining strength, and the park closed for good in the late 1920s. The land was divided into lots and sold for new homes.

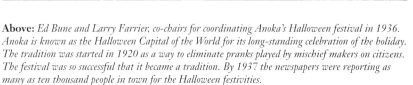

Above: *Ed Bune and Larry Farrier, co-chairs for coordinating Anoka's Halloween festival in 1936. Anoka is known as the Halloween Capital of the World for its long-standing celebration of the holiday. The tradition was started in 1920 as a way to eliminate pranks played by mischief makers on citizens. The festival was so successful that it became a tradition. By 1937 the newspapers were reporting as many as ten thousand people in town for the Halloween festivities.*

Top left: *The "Pumpkin Bowl" football game, featuring the Anoka High School Tornados, is always a part of the Halloween festivities. Audrey Gow was the Homecoming Queen in 1953 and rode in the Grand Day Parade on the Saturday closest to the actual date of Halloween.*

Top middle: *Hilltop's parade float, pictured here sometime in the 1990s, has been included in Columbia Heights' Jamboree since the early 1970s.*

Top right: *The East Bethel Seniors put together this float for the St. Francis Pioneer Days Parade in 1997. Their theme was "You can't leave home without it" and featured many of their members with various musical instruments—homemade or otherwise.*

Right: *Halloween in Anoka has included as many as three parades each year. This float participated in the "Big Parade of Little People" in 1991 and was the signature float for the city that year. Miss Anoka, Kristin Young, is seated on the top. Princess Jennifer Foss is in front.*

Top and middle left: *Santa Claus Town, a classic 1953 roadside attraction, was built by Bernard Swanson of Anoka for his children. The attraction was on an eight-acre site just outside the Anoka city limits in Ramsey and right on Highway 10. The former industrial engineer from Brainerd did most of the work himself, creating not only a summer home for Santa, but a miniature electric railroad, Mother Goose and Bible characters, rides, concession stands, a picnic ground, playground, and more. One of the highlights of the park was the electric train that was rebuilt from a mining locomotive used in an underground mine near Hibbing. It became the Story Book Train with the help of Russell Swearingen, who operated the train. It ran on two banks of batteries and could carry as many as seventy-two children all day on a single charge. Santa Claus Town did not last long. The figures were sold in 1960.*

Middle right: *Greenhaven Golf Course ca. 1940, Anoka. Opened in 1937, it was originally a nine-hole course on 102 acres. Besides golf, the grounds at one time featured skeet and trap shooting and four bowling alleys.*

Right: *65 Hi Drive-In Theater sign, 2002. Drive-ins got their start on the East Coast in the 1930s and moved west. In the 1950s, the country's love affairs with cars and films found a perfect match at the outdoor theaters. By the 1960s, drive-ins had gained a salacious reputation because of the relative privacy the automobiles offered patrons. Many drive-ins survived into the 1980s catering to niche audiences. In Anoka County, as with the rest of the country, the encroaching suburbs eventually claimed many of the drive-ins as land became more valuable than the business. The 65 Hi Drive-In, located in Blaine, lost out to townhomes. Similar fates happened to drive-ins in Fridley, Coon Rapids, and Columbia Heights.*

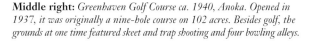

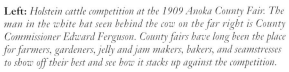

Left: *Holstein cattle competition at the 1909 Anoka County Fair. The man in the white hat seen behind the cow on the far right is County Commissioner Edward Ferguson. County fairs have long been the place for farmers, gardeners, jelly and jam makers, bakers, and seamstresses to show off their best and see how it stacks up against the competition.*

Middle left: *Many children were taught to swim by Les Mason, who also coached the Anoka High School football team. Lessons, first offered in 1931, were sponsored by the Red Cross and, later, the Anoka Park Board and the American Legion and auxiliary.*

Middle right: *Cub Scouts carried the American flag to lead off the Kiddie Parade at the Linwood Family Fun Fest in September 1991. The parade ran through the parking lot of the Linwood Town Hall.*

Bottom: *The Bunker Beach Water Park's wave pool under construction in 1987 and on its opening day in 1988. The pool remains a featured attraction at the park. Operated by the Anoka County Department of Parks and Recreation, it is 25,000 square feet, and the water temperature is always a comfortable 73 degrees.*

Left: *Entrance to the Carlos Avery Game Farm, Columbus, ca. 1992, named for Carlos Avery, Minnesota's first conservation commissioner. The state purchased the property in 1933 and opened it as a game farm in 1937. It was considered one of the most modern and complete ones of its kind and received universal praise from conservationists. Between 1936 and 1938, the Works Progress Administration constructed administrative buildings. Placed on the National Register of Historic Places in 1990, the game farm is also infamous for being the location of the final shootout between the O'Kasick brothers and the Anoka County Sheriff's Department in 1957. The incident resulted in the deaths of two of the three O'Kasick brothers and Eugene Lindstrom, their hostage.*

Middle: *The 1921 Anoka County Fair featured a motorcycle race. The racer on the far left of the track is H. T. Hanson, who was a deputy county sheriff.*

Bottom: *1952 Soderville Baseball Team. Front row: (l-r) Dave Williams, Gary Rognrud. Middle row: (l-r) Dick Johnson, Harvey Peterson, Dave Spencer, Frank Larson, Quent Peterson, Norb Koch, Danny Anderson. Back row: (l-r) Fuddy Hendrickson, Bobo Marchiniaic, Larry Winkler, Phil Butler, George Masko, Tony Johnson, Bob Paquin, Bud McPhearson. A group of teenage boys from the Johnsville area (in what is now Ham Lake), started the team in the 1940s. They raised money for equipment by collecting and selling scrap iron. Their first uniforms were T-shirts with "Johnsville" printed across the chest. Later, after they received local business sponsorships to furnish uniforms, they changed the name to the Soderville Orioles.*

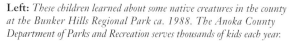

Left: *These children learned about some native creatures in the county at the Bunker Hills Regional Park ca. 1988. The Anoka County Department of Parks and Recreation serves thousands of kids each year.*

Middle left: *Volunteers putting the finishing touches on Hilltop's playground, 1996. To celebrate its fortieth anniversary, the tiny community, average population fewer than one thousand, came together to build a playground for its youngest residents.*

Middle right: *Golden Lake has long been a favorite spot on a hot summer day, though the poses of these young swimmers might indicate the swimming lesson that day was a cold one.*

Bottom: *These boys, photographed in the mid-1970s, were just one more generation of Anoka County residents to catch fish in the Rum River. The river has supplied many meals to hungry families from present day to the Native American families of the distant past.*

8

Coming Together:
Anoka County in the Face of Disaster

*D*isaster is about the most opposite one can get from fun. Yet, both have a place in Anoka County's 150-year history. Last chapter, we saw the fun side of the county's history. This chapter shows us some of the disasters residents have dealt with.

Tornadoes are fairly common in the Upper Midwest, but Anoka County dealt with some devastating tornadoes in the past sixty plus years. One deadly storm was the 1939 tornado that ripped through Anoka.

A quarter-century later, in 1965, several tornadoes attacked the county. One hit Fridley, Spring Lake Park, and Blaine. Another hit Centerville. That horrific night, several tornadoes beat up Minnesota, but Anoka County took the hardest punch.

Another weather disaster came most springs in the form of flooding in Anoka. That was no surprise since the Rum and Mississippi Rivers come together in Anoka, but it was still hard to watch the water rise and rush into people's homes along the beautiful river fronts.

Nature, not weather, caused one of the worst disaster farmers faced in the 1930s. Grasshopper plagues destroyed crops, compromised the land, and ruined farmers.

Train wrecks reminded residents how times were changing and speeding up. The county had its share of them.

Fires always meant disaster to early county residents, but Anoka's fire in 1884 decimated the downtown business district.

The Cargill plant explosion in Columbia Heights in 1955 tossed men through walls, but no one was killed.

The county has faced many tests of its resolve and always survived whatever disaster came its way. Perhaps that is one of the best lessons history can teach us: don't give up; a brighter day is coming, and we do survive.

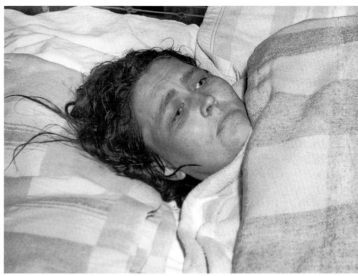

Top left: *Aftermath of the 1939 tornado's destruction of the Anoka Armory. Anoka, placed where the Rum and Mississippi Rivers meet, always believed it was safe until June 18, 1939, when a devastating tornado tore apart many city blocks and killed nine people and left hundreds homeless.*

Top right: *A traumatized victim of the 1939 Anoka tornado.*

Bottom: *A bird's-eye view of Fridley's devastation by the 1965 tornado. The southern portion of Anoka County took the brunt of storms and tornadoes on May 6, 1965. Three people were killed, and 175 more were injured in one tornado that cut through Fridley, Spring Lake Park, and Blaine. A second tornado moved from Fridley, across a corner of Ramsey County, and came back through Centerville before dissipating. By the time it was through, it had killed six people and injured 158. Four other tornados touched down in other parts of Minnesota, all part of the same storm system.*

Top: *Farmer with poison bait for grasshoppers. The 1930s were a high point for grasshoppers in Anoka County, with the potential for eggs hatching at more than 200 grasshoppers per square foot. To control the grasshopper population, farmers created a poison bait by mixing sawdust, bran, and sodium arsenate. The bran was the "bait" to entice the grasshoppers to eat it so the sodium arsenate could kill them. Two mixing stations were set up in the county in 1937, and within just a few days, 115 tons of poison bait was produced. Thanks to the hard work and widespread efforts the year before, 1939 saw only a few localized infestations of grasshoppers. Still, farmers were taking no chances. They spread 215 tons of bait on about 250 farms. It was estimated they saved about $150,000 worth of crops that season by spending just $565 on baiting efforts.*

Middle: *Train wrecks were a reality of an industrial age, and Anoka County was not spared. This photo depicts a wreck near the boundary between Anoka and Coon Rapids ca. 1940. The wrecks were common enough that folklore gave rise to the tale of the city of Andover's naming. Legend has it that a train, after skipping the tracks, rolled over and over. Thus, Andover! There is no factual evidence to support this story, but it makes for a great tale.*

Bottom: *Launching a boat from a flooded city sidewalk in Anoka near Second Avenue. This lower area was susceptible to severe flooding from the Rum River. Recently, fill raised the area to a safer level for housing.*

Top: *Photo shows the total loss of the Anoka National Bank at the corner of First and Main. The fire, believed to have started in an outbuilding behind the school on Monroe Street, consumed the majority of downtown Anoka on August 16, 1884. Fires were common prior to 1884, but after this one, much of the business district was rebuilt with brick construction. Citizens paid closer attention to fire safety with implementation of fire codes.*

Middle and bottom: *History repeated itself when the Colburn-Hilliard Store burned on the same block in 1948 despite the brick and fire codes. Just as in 1884, spectators gathered to watch the 1948 fire.*

On February 14, 1955, the Cargill Plant, at 3700 Fifth Street NE in Columbia Heights, exploded. According to the Columbia Heights Record, *witnesses described a sound "like an atomic bomb." Employees were blown through the walls of the plant. Fourteen were injured, but none were killed. The plant extracted linseed oil.*

9

The Soul of the County:
Anoka County People and Their Organizations

It's impossible to acknowledge every person and every organization that contributed to the 150 years of Anoka County's historical journey. Many anonymous residents went about their daily routines, making sure life went on. Others took leadership roles, and their names made the news. Still others are known because they owned businesses, made the social pages, or somehow found their names recorded in journals or letters.

The pictures in this chapter barely scratch the surface of who and what made Anoka County the wonderful place it is. Look at each photo. Read each caption. Then make sure you keep your own family history so future historians can see history through your eyes.

One of the most important organizations in history is the church. You'll see a 1900 congregation witness immersion baptism in the Rum River near St. Francis. And the aftermath of a 1949 fire in Columbia Heights' Methodist church. And children in Sunday school and churches across the county.

And you'll want to see the pictures of the Agriculture Extension Service, the Boy Scouts, the Girl Scouts, and the community organizations from Burns and Linwood.

Beyond the organizations are the people. Interesting people do interesting things and have interesting stories.

We're at the end of our 150-year history of Anoka County. Now it's time to start writing the next installment for future historians. History is story, but history is fleeting. If we don't capture it today, it will be lost as history tomorrow. We've enjoyed what the previous generations left us. Let's give the same enjoyment to future generations. Save your history.

Top left: *The Rum River in St. Francis was the setting for a baptism by immersion about 1900. The congregation can be seen gathered on the river bank with the mill in the background.*

Top right: *Our Savior's Lutheran Church was established on Swedish Drive in Ham Lake and was commonly known as the Swedish Lutheran church. This house was used as the parsonage—the residence of the pastor—but it was owned by the church.*

Middle left: *St. Patrick's Catholic Church in Oak Grove was established and built in 1862. It served its congregation until the parish moved to a new building in 1976.*

Middle right: *The House of Praise Church in Lino Lakes, shown in 1992, has made creative reuse of an older building. The church is located on County Road 14 west of Lake Drive.*

Left: *The Methodist Church in Columbia Heights suffered considerable damage from a fire in 1949. Firefighters put it out, and the congregation rebuilt.*

Top left: *These children were part of Myrtle Hendrickson's Sunday school class at the Hope Presbyterian Church in Columbus. Included in this photo are: George E. Grubbs, Steve LeVesseur, Gordon Newell, Agnes Hendrickson, Dorothy (Grubbs) Muller, Virgie Newell, and Gladyce Hendrickson.*

Top right: *St. Joseph's Catholic Church of Lino Lakes shown in 1978. First incorporated as a parish in 1891, at that time it was known as the Rice Lake Church and was in Centerville Township. It was considered a mission church from the St. Genevieve Catholic Church in Centerville. The Rice Lake Church, a wooden structure, was destroyed by a tornado in the first years of its existence. The church was rebuilt with brick in 1896 and is the one pictured here. In 1939, St. Joseph's became a parish of its own. Before then all records were kept at Centerville since St. Joseph's was considered a mission church. Father Francis Hamming was the first pastor, serving until his death in 1945. In June 1963, a new church building was completed next to the old one. The new church could hold seven hundred people for services and other activities. The old church, originally built to accommodate 130 people, continued to be used for daily Mass and for weddings and funerals. By 2004 extensive work was under way to restore the old church to its former appearance inside.*

Bottom left: *The Church of St. Genevieve of Paris, shown in 1991, began in the home of Francis LaMotte in the early 1850s. It has had three buildings; this is the third, constructed in 1904.*

Bottom right: *Passing on their faith and traditions have been of key importance in county churches. These children are part of a Bible class at Our Savior's Lutheran Church in Ham Lake, 1965. Luther Hall was a small building used for education.*

Right: *Having your "likeness" made was quite the thing in the early years of photography. Olaf and Mathilda Erickson of East Bethel brought out the fainting couch and posed their horses as well for their family portrait about 1891. Standing (l-r) are Otto, Wally, and Olaf Erickson, and Gustaf Magnuson, who was the father of Mathilda. Seated are George, Mrs. W. Munson, Elmer, and Mathilda, with Jenny on her lap.*

Middle left: *A gathering of neighbors in the Linwood area organized into what soon took the name Helping Hands Club. The club had dues and held fundraisers to provide funds for their good-works projects in the community. The club was quite vital to the social network in Linwood. This photo was taken in 1996 at the one hundredth birthday of the Linwood club.*

Middle right: *These smiling ladies ca. 1920s are members of the Neighborhood Social Club of Burns Township. Left to right: Gerty Wirz, Annie Wirz, Laura Wirz, Mrs. N. A. Anderson, Eva Colburn, and Alvina Wirz. The photo was taken by member Niami M. Eann.*

Bottom: *The Bethel Brass Band was a lively group of musicians including Tom Clarkson, Guy Cooper, Ed Sam, S. T. Nelson, G. C. Lambert, Alfred Meers, Nels Wicklander, Elijah Mitchell, Lloyd Odenwald, Elwood King, Ralph Odenwald, George Barcelou, and Napoleon Young.*

Sinclair Gasoline, in Fridley Township (now Hilltop), and views of the Trailer City Park in 1952. In 1948 Les Johnson purchased the store from Dr. Good. Les and Mary Ann Johnson lived on the second floor with their family. These photos were taken for a court case in which the county wanted to obtain the land and compensate the Johnsons as though the land were empty and used for growing potatoes.

The tiny community of Hilltop has a story unlike most others. Completely enclosed within the city of Columbia Heights, it is an incorporated city of a mere sixteen square blocks. Most of its housing consists of trailer homes in four parks. When Hilltop was part of Fridley Township in the mid-1950s, the residents of the four parks, concerned that the township intended to remove their parks, proposed that Columbia Heights annex the four parks. The request was declined, and Les Johnson, owner of one of the parks, circulated a petition to the parks' residents to incorporate as a city. On May 1, 1956, the residents passed the measure to create the City of Hilltop. In the years that followed, Columbia Heights annexed the land surrounding Hilltop, and a period of contentiousness developed between the two cities. In 1968 the two city councils, led by Hilltop Mayor Vivian Caesar and Columbia Heights Mayor Bruce Nawrocki, came together to discuss their differences and how they could be resolved. It was the beginning of a new era of communication between the neighboring communities.

Top left: *The five oldest sons of Olaf and Christine Peterson were hired in 1898 by the Palace Museum in Minneapolis to appear on stage as "The Tall Men." The young men were paid sixty dollars a week for their appearances. Oscar, the youngest, did not get hired, as he was sixteen at the time and stood only 6 feet tall. The other brothers averaged 6-foot-4. They toured the state, performing feats of strength such as chopping logs and lifting giant weights.*

Top middle: *James Hare, the man credited with giving Nowthen its name. It all started in 1878 when Burns Township wanted to have a post office, but the Postal Department refused the use of the name Burns as it was already in use by another post office in Minnesota. Names were suggested at a meeting, and Hare was to write the letter to the Postal Department with the list. He listed several suggested names, then concluded the letter with one of his favorite sayings, "Nowthen . . . ." When the approval came from the department, the name of the new post office in Burns was "Nowthen." Though never incorporated as its own community, Nowthen remains a well known place in Anoka County.*

Top right: *Henry C. Rehbien, pictured in 1969, was born on land that would become Lino Lakes in 1893, and though he lived several places in the community, it remained his home throughout his life. He served in WWI and built a home with his wife and two daughters near what is now Birch Street in Lino Lakes. The area was tree-covered, so wood provided heating and cooking energy. The family had some dairy cows and raised vegetables to sell. Henry died in 1970.*

Bottom left and right: *On November 21, 1881, Samuel and Louise Wirz were married in Gelterkinder, Switzerland. Seeking better opportunities, the couple and their infant daughter made the long journey to Anoka County, Minnesota, arriving in 1883. Both of them took jobs, and through hard work and careful economy, they were able to buy a farm in Burns Township. Though their first baby died, the Wirzes raised five sons and a daughter. Those children grew up, married, and had children of their own, who also grew up. When Sam and Louise celebrated their sixtieth wedding anniversary in 1941, there were at least sixty-seven Wirz family members living in the nearby area. They gathered to take a family portrait on the occasion, proof of the "good seed" planted by Samuel and Louise so many years earlier when they arrived in Anoka County.*

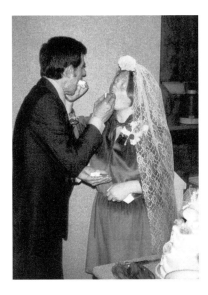

Top left and middle: *Steve and Carol Huntsperger are institutions at Northtown Mall in Blaine, having been married in the mall's community room in 1983. Steve has been working for the mall since 1979, and Carol has been there since 1986. After meeting on the bus in 1979, the pair went on their first date at Woolworth's, also in the mall. These photos show Steve and Carol at their wedding April 30, 1983, and Steve training for employment under the direction of Gary Valley, 1979.*

Top right: *Margaret Langfeld was the first woman to serve as Anoka County Board chair, a term she began in 2005. She and Natalie Haas were the first two women to serve on the county board when they were both elected in 1982.*

Bottom left: *In 1994 John and Jill Weaver (with Garrison Keillor, right, popular radio host and author) hosted the kickoff event for the Anoka County Historical Society's (ACHS) fund drive to find a new home. Keillor put on a benefit performance at the Fred Moore Middle School, which served as Anoka's high school when he graduated in 1960. Afterwards, a reception was held at the historic Weaver home on Ferry Street in Anoka.*

Bottom right: *Eight years later, as a result of the successful fund drive, the Historical Society opened the doors to its new home, the Anoka County History Center and Library, in the former city library building at 2135 Third Avenue North in Anoka. The Historical Society, founded in 1934, is dedicated to interpreting and preserving the county's history. Seen here left to right, are Richard Sorenson, 1942 recipient of the Congressional Medal of Honor; Nina Archibal, executive director of the Minnesota Historical Society; and John Weaver, president of the Anoka County Historical Society. They are pictured here cutting the ribbon on the History Center on July 13, 2002.*

Index

About the Author

Sharron Stockhausen has written a weekly newspaper column on Anoka County history since 1995. She has authored or co-authored seven books and teaches in the Graduate School of Management at Hamline University and in the College of Management at Metropolitan State University. She also teaches courses on writing and publishing for Minnesota State Colleges and Universities (MNSCU). She has served in every position on the Anoka County Board of Directors except president. She is CEO of Expert Publishing Inc. and owns Stockhausen Ink, a communications consulting firm. Sharron holds a master's degree in management and administration and a bachelor's degree in business. She has two grown children and lives with her husband, Harry, in Andover, Minnesota.

About the Photo Editors

Todd Mahon has been the Executive Director of the Anoka County Historical Society since December 2005. He graduated cum laude and with departmental honors in 1998 from Hamline University with a bachelor's degree in history. He is currently finishing a master's in Public and Nonprofit Administration from Metropolitan State University. Prior to working with ACHS, he worked with the Minnesota Historical Society, the Kautz Family YMCA Archives of the University of Minnesota, and the Hennepin History Museum—where his work was given national recognition from the American Association for State and Local History.

Vickie Wendel began with the Anoka County Historical Society as a volunteer in 1987 and joined the staff in 1989 as a tour guide. In 1994 she and Jean Smith served as co-directors of ACHS before Vickie transitioned into focusing on outreach, exhibits, and programs as the Program Manager. A resident of Anoka County since the age of eleven (save for the few years her husband served in the military), Vickie holds a bachelor's degree from Metropolitan State University in American History with a special focus on the Civil War.